ROGER BANNISTER AND THE FOUR-MINUTE MILE

On 6 May 1954, in what is regarded as one of the key moments in the history of modern sport, Roger Bannister became the first person to run a mile in under four minutes. Fifty years on, Bannister's status, not just as a champion athlete but also as a true British hero, a gentleman and an amateur from a 'golden era' in sport, retains its unblemished appeal.

Until now there has been little critical and even less close historical study of Bannister and his achievement. This book redresses the balance, and in doing so provides fresh insights into the making of this British champion.

Roger Bannister and the Four-Minute Mile does more than detail the history of a sports star. It is a testimonial to the legend of Roger Bannister but it also invites the reader to reconsider the very words often used to describe him – notably 'hero' and 'gentleman amateur'. Informed by contemporary sports science, the text also questions the significance of the four-minute mile *per se*.

Thoroughly researched, this book gives fascinating insights into the history of track racing as well as early athletic training methods and the beginnings of sports science.

The first rigorous historical study of Bannister's sporting life and the man behind the legend reveals an ambivalent athlete – highly achievement-orientated and scientific in his approach but also in love with the freedom of running sensuously in nature, in contrast to the constraints of modern sport.

John Bale divides his time researching and teaching between the University of Aarhus, Denmark and Keele University, UK. He is also author of *Imagined Olympians* (University of Minnesota Press) and *Running Cultures* (Routledge).

ROGER BANNISTER AND THE FOUR-MINUTE MILE

Sports Myth and Sports History

JOHN BALE

Routledge
Taylor & Francis Group

LONDON AND NEW YORK

First published 2004
by Routledge
2 Park Square, Milton Park, Abingdon, Oxon OX14 4RN

Simultaneously published in the USA and Canada
by Taylor & Francis Inc
270 Madison Ave, New York, NY10016

This edition published in paperback 2005

Routledge is an imprint of the Taylor & Francis Group

© 2004, 2005 John Bale

Typeset in Joanna by
HWA Text and Data Management, Tunbridge Wells
Printed and bound in Great Britain by
TJ International, Padstow, Cornwall

Every effort has been made to ensure that the advice and
information in this book is true and accurate at the time of going
to press. However, neither the publisher nor the author can
accept any legal responsibility or liability for any errors or
omissions that may be made.

British Library Cataloguing in Publication Data
A catalogue record for this book is available from the British
Library

Library of Congress Cataloging in Publication Data
A catalog record for this book has been requested

ISBN 0–415–34606–1 (hb)
ISBN 0–415–34607–X (pb)

FOR NIELS AND BRITA, WITH THANKS

CONTENTS

LIST OF ILLUSTRATIONS

FIGURES

TABLES

ACKNOWLEDGEMENTS

In writing this book I have been helped by a number of friends and colleagues. I must thank Murray Phillips and Anthony Bale for reading and commenting constructively on various versions of the text. Also, I am very grateful for the supply of sources, ideas and facts that would have otherwise eluded me and that have been provided by Rebecca Abbott, Pat Clohessy, Les Crouch, Jim Denison, Ian Jobling, John Hoberman, Stuart Jeffries, Peter Mewett, Tim Phillips and Bob Phillips. The book was more or less completed while I was a guest of the School of Human Movement Studies at the University of Queensland. I am grateful to Richard Tinning and Bruce Abernathy for facilitating a visiting professorship and for providing a stimulating and friendly milieu where I could carry out my last minute scribbling. The coffee-break-seminars are sadly missed. While writing this book I have also benefited from the support of colleagues at the Centre for Sports Studies at the University of Aarhus.

I would like to thank Samantha Grant, Allison Scott and Jonathan Manley at Routledge. They provided an unusual degree of support, advice and assistance in the book's production. I am also grateful for permission to reproduce photographs, the sources of which are acknowledged in their respective captions. It has been impossible to contact one or two copyright holders and if any omissions can be located I will be happy to include them in subsequent printings of this work.

Although many people contributed to the pages that follow, any 'factual' errors are mine alone.

John Bale

Aarhus

We are the weary, who begin
    The race with joy, but early fail,
Because we do not care to win
    A race that goes not to the frail
And humble: only the proud come in.
                                    Charles Hamilton Sorley

I

A SPORTING HERO?

Somewhere in the cavalcade of British sports heroes there is Roger
Bannister who, on 6 May 1954, as almost everyone of a certain age
(interested in sport or not) knows, was recorded as being the first man
to run a mile in less than four minutes. This performance is widely
regarded as one of 'the really important moments in sport', one of
'the great first achievements which seem to open up new worlds of
human possibility'. Such an achievement creates the sporting hero,
sustained by our fantasy and desire. Garry Whannel, Media Studies
expert, suggests that sports heroes are either 'good boys', 'pretty boys'
or 'bad boys'; Roger Bannister is included among his 'good boys'. His
'goodness' has often been seen as his embodiment of the English
gentleman, and a gentleman of a particular kind – the sporting
gentleman, the 'gentleman amateur', the sort of fellow championed in
Chariots of Fire. Bannister has also been described as a throwback to the
heyday of the Amateur Athletics Association (AAA) which, presumably,
places emphasis on the amateur, the lover of running, for its own sake.
The word 'amateur' also carries connotations of not taking things too
seriously, a good sport, not training too hard, certainly no cash involved,
having more in life than one's sport. This, suggests Lincoln Allison in

his book, *Amateurism in Sport*, makes up the 'Roger Bannister Syndrome', at the heart of which is, well, heart. It is the image of an athlete who is as honest as the day is long, an educated man of independent means, hence upper class, exhausting himself to break the world's record but, at the same time, believing that winning was neither everything nor the only thing.

As Allison observes, such heroics need no sales pitch. Bannister's brand of hero was, indeed, resolutely anti-commercial, and he was certainly not a celebrity. Even so, it is wise for Allison to call the Bannister Syndrome an 'image', something that comes from somewhere, is constructed, communicated, received and internalised. A key objective of this book is to examine and contest this image.

Bannister has been represented as a hero, or someone held in high esteem – at least for some people – because he broke what was thought to be the most celebrated of all athletic barriers, the four-minute mile. Regarded variously as both a physical and psychological 'barrier', his breaking through this perceived wall of time has been called the sublime achievement in British athletics.

POST-IMPERIAL, POST-WAR AND THE MILE

The contents of the following pages are mainly about the 1950s, a decade of imperial measures but also of imperial decline. According to Whannel, Bannister's four-minute mile 'became a potent national symbol against the perceived loss of national prowess'. In 1954 Bannister's mile was seen as equalling in significance the conquest of Mount Everest, just over a year earlier by Tenzing Norgay and Edmund Hillary, led (of course, but not conquered) by the Englishman, John Hunt. Historian Richard Holt sees both events as giving the nation hope for the future in the wider post-imperial world, following the coronation of Queen Elizabeth II. Put another way, Bannister's achievement was presented as a British achievement, the body of the athlete reflecting the body politic. Roger Bannister was seen as doing it for Britain (even if he was really doing it for himself) as a 'new Elizabethan'; it was that, too, that made him a hero – not just a hero, a national hero. Britannia had suffered during the Second World War but she could still rule the world, at least on the running track. We did it first.

The four-minute mile wasn't only a post-colonial boost for Britain. It came at a time of post-war austerity, the Cold War menace, a time when the country needed bucking up. National well-being through sporting achievements was said to be well typified in 1954; besides Bannister there was Diane Leather, becoming the first woman to break five minutes for the mile and Bannister's Oxford friend, Chris Chataway, breaking the world 5,000 metres record and in classic Cold War fashion, in the process beating the Soviet sailor Vladimir Kuts (who was soon to reclaim the world record). Needless to say, the efforts of neither Leather nor Chataway matched the impact of Bannister's achievement. However, the proportion of the population who really did feel bucked-up as a result of these, and other such performances, is simply unknown.

To be sure, the four-minute mile took some beating and some athletes, trainers and coaches, as late as the 1930s and 1940s, thought it was impossible. But because it had been talked about since the turn of the century, demand for the four-minute mile was high. As early as 1904 the Harvard scientist, Arthur E. Kennelly, had predicted that the mile could be run in 3 minutes 58 seconds, but others thought that such a prognostication was sheer fantasy. The American scientist, G.P. Meade felt that the possibility of a 'natural miler' running four minutes was 'beyond the realms of reason'. Given such incredulity, or given that it had long been predicted, the first man to attain it would certainly be held in high esteem – a hero. The delivery, and the subsequent increase in the supply of four-minute miles after May 1954 meant that the amount of esteem fell substantially for those who then ran it. How many readers of this book know the name of the third – even the second – four-minute miler?

If track fans had been aware of the numerous statistical predictions that had been published, they could have known when the four-minute mile was likely to happen. A recent study, by the late track and field fanatic Alphonse Juilland, traced the trajectory of the world mile record from 1930 to 1950. He found out that on 6 May 1954 the record should have been a smidgen outside four minutes. For many, one of the mystical aspects of the four-minute mile was that it had taken so long to achieve but using the same model Juilland predicted that the first four-minute mile should not have happened until May 1955. Bannister's result, therefore, was ahead of its time, at least according to Juilland's model. On the other hand, as I shall show later, with the benefit of hindsight other followers of athletics are almost certain that the 'dream mile' could have been achieved in the 1940s, a decade before Bannister's well-known run.

For much of the first half of the twentieth century, running tracks varied in size. Yet the mile, whether it was run over three or four laps, possessed a certain mystique. While the mile is an imperial measure, those who used the metric system in their daily lives also understood the idea of the 'English mile' when it came to foot-racing. The mile was neither too long nor too short; running it was neither too fast nor too slow. And by the 1950s, when the size of tracks had become increasingly standardised at 440 yards (or 400 metres), the four-minute mile had become a neat and tidy barrier, alliterative and symmetrical, a neat relation of time and space (four minutes, four laps). Reporting on the four-minute mile, the athletics correspondent of The Times suggested that the 'fascination of the round figure which conveys to everyone a sense of real achievement no doubt is one of the reasons why the four-minute mile has captured the popular imagination'. It was like the 10 second 100 yards, or later, the 10 second 100 meters – even time – where a yard or a metre per second were easily comprehensible to both fan and fanatic alike. With the four-minute mile set at four laps at a minute per lap it was a rather special kind of record breaking, so special that it would bring lasting fame. An Olympic title is generally thought to be of some permanence, to be remembered by the public long after the medal has been won. The cliché is that a record can be taken from one whereas an Olympic title lasts for ever. But this particular 'record' lasted by means of myth and romanticism.

But pause for a moment to think about it: A quarter of a mile run in one minute, followed by three more without a break to catch your breath. In most high schools today there will only be one or two kids who can run a quarter-mile – or 400 metres – in a minute.

BANNISTER AS GENTLEMAN

Bannister's heroic status has hardly been built on a 'rags to riches' scenario. The general impression is that he is upper class – the 'gentleman amateur' breaking the previously impenetrable barrier. Yet Roger Bannister's origins were relatively humble – in his own words, he had 'a simple origin, without any great privilege'. Some privilege, perhaps, but not as much as many of the people with whom he would later rub shoulders. Ralph Bannister, his father, was one of 11 children and born near Colne in Lancashire, his family having lived in the same village for 400 years. At Colne Secondary School he liked sports and won the school mile championship. While never carrying on running, he did retain an interest in sport. Ralph had ambition, however, and passed a nationwide Civil Service examination. As a result, he moved to London, working as a civil servant at the Treasury and living in the northern suburb of Harrow. It was here that his second child, Roger Gilbert Bannister, was born on 23 March 1929 and where he was brought up.

Alice Bannister, Roger's mother, had worked in a cotton mill until she was in her late teens but she later qualified as a schoolteacher, though never took a job in teaching. She had middle-class aspirations and furthered her own education by reading. She put a strong emphasis on education for her two children and there were plenty of books to be found in the family residence. And in the best protestant tradition, which may well have carried over into his later exploits as a runner, young Roger was brought up to regard wasting time as a crime. The Bannisters were sufficiently well-off for Alice not to have to take a job outside the home. So, Roger Bannister's parents were middle class – teacher and civil servant living in Harrow – suburban, leafy avenues, beloved by poet John Betjeman, on the Metropolitan line, on the 'right side of the tracks'.

With Ralph Bannister working in a government office and with the onset of war the Bannisters moved to Bath. Here Roger started his secondary education, most of which was at the City of Bath Boys' School, a state grammar school that today is a comprehensive. Here he passed the matriculation examination to enter the sixth form. He was a serious scholar, working hard and showing an interest in all subjects. Roger Bannister later described this period of his life as one where 'the exciting prospect of war for a ten-year-old turned into a bewildering succession of air-raid warnings, evacuation, and broken schooling'. Returning to London after the war he attended, for a short period, the nineteenth-century University College School at Hampstead, a liberal independent day school but hardly a 'public school' in the traditions of Eton or Harrow, Winchester or Marlborough.

That's some of the family background. Knowing this, Roger Bannister doesn't quite look like the 'English gentleman' described earlier. Middle class, yes, aristocracy, certainly not. I will make further revisions to the generally accepted image of Bannister later but, for the moment, proceed to supply some more background.

His secondary education completed, he moved on, attending two colleges at Oxford University; first, Exeter as an undergraduate where, he tells us, 'money was tight', and then, as a postgraduate, at Merton. Following five years at Oxford he then did his medical training at St Mary's Hospital, London, and later became a well-respected neurologist, a medical man publishing articles on the physiology of exercise, heat illness and various neurological subjects. He was the first chairman of the Sports Council (1976–83), and in his later life returned to Oxford as Master of Pembroke College (1985–93). He had retired from serious, competitive running when he was 25. What a life! Yet most people remember him as the four-minute miler.

It is Roger Bannister's life as a runner, its context, and his engagement with running that form the focal points of this short book. I try not to burden the reader with too many statistics, facts and figures. This book is not a gazetteer of results. It is not just a description of events or a catalogue of 'what happened'. Nor is it my intention to write, to any extent, Bannister's life beyond the world of running.

As a teenager he had applied to Cambridge, but they wanted him to wait a year so he entered Oxford University at the age of 17. At that time only about three per cent of the population went to university, never mind Oxford or Cambridge. Almost 90 per cent of the students were men and Bannister said that they 'came from more of a public school background than I did' (emphasising the distance between University College School and, say, Eton). Public schools were places for toffs. Bannister was a scholarship boy. If the average person in Britain in 1946 had any image of Oxford it was probably one that included the boat race or of students who were snobs wearing gowns and having tea and crumpets in their college rooms, looked after by their 'scouts' (as the curious Oxford dialect would have it). Then there were May Balls, rugger balls, jumping off Magdalen Bridge into the river on May Morning, punting on the Cherwell.

Some people may have known that in addition to Oxford's rowing kudos it also had something of a reputation for athletics and for being the *alma mater* of several famous runners. Additionally, the AAA had been founded in Oxford in 1880 when 28 sporting worthies assembled at the Randolph Hotel. Today, in the Morse Bar, a plaque commemorates the meeting. And then there were the athletes. For a start, there was Jack Lovelock, the Rhodes scholar from New Zealand, and winner of the 1,500 metres at the Nazi Olympics in 1936 (he hardly considered not attending). Less well-known Olympic winners who had been Oxford men included Arnold Strode Jackson, winner of the 1,500 metres in 1912; Douglas Lowe, winner of the 800 at both the 1924 and 1928 Games and Tom Hampson, winner of the same event at Los Angeles in 1932 – and that's only the *gold* medallists.

Given this image of Oxford, and the identification of Bannister with it, may make it rather surprising that Bannister has been represented as a *popular* hero. After all, social psychologists tell us that individuals tend to be attracted to those who have similar characteristics and backgrounds and as I will show, he was not universally admired. The question of *how* heroic is a hero is rarely raised yet it is clear that not everyone necessarily finds a hero in a star, a champion, or a record holder. As I shall show, for some people, Bannister had not done quite enough to be heroic.

However, Bannister did appear to possess the attributes of the Englishman, *par excellence*. Certainly a good boy, clean and decent, tall – in his prime six feet two inches and 11 stones – blond and slim, athletic, almost Aryan, every parent's favourite son; yet somehow also vulnerable, almost ascetic, with his thin face, high cheekbones and lank hair (see Figure 1.1). There was no scandal about him that the public knew of. That typified 'bad boy' heroes. And his relationship with Shirley Williams (later a Labour MP, then one of the 'gang of four' who started the short-lived Social Democrats, and is currently the Liberal Democrat leader in the House of Lords) in the early 1950s hardly amounted to

Figure 1.1 Roger Bannister with his parents and sister, Harrow, 1954
(*Illustrated London News* Picture Library)

anything more than a fling – more like a 'flingette' – and, as far as I know, was not publicised until it was mentioned, in passing, in *The Guardian* a few years ago.

But when we use words like 'hero', 'gentleman', 'amateur' and even 'four-minute mile', do we really *know* what we are talking about? Are the words as transparent as they might, at first, seem? I will show later how the word 'amateur' is a complex, multi-faceted term and that Bannister embodied some aspects of the 'amateur' but not others. I have already shown how the 'meaning' of the word 'gentleman' changes slightly when we know a little more about Bannister's background. Fifty years on from the first four-minute mile, I suggest that Roger Bannister is a figure worthy of re-evaluation, as is the evolving world mile record. As Chris Healy has observed, memorable events (like the four-minute mile) that endure, 'even though they may ossify over the years and become predictable, are never quite as safe as they appear'. The fact that images are created at certain points in time is an invitation to revise them later. This can be done by reading between the lines of the records written 50 years ago, by drawing on what preceded those events and what has followed them. This is, then, a short revisionist history of Sir Roger's running career and the ever-shifting horizon of the record.

REVISIONING ROGER

Before continuing I think it would be useful to define what I mean by a 'revisionist' view. As the word implies, it simply involves revising history and, though the word has assumed some negative connotations, there is nothing intrinsically wrong with it. It is simply challenging accepted descriptions, causes and consequences of historical representations. I will not dispute certain facts. Roger Bannister is a real person and he did, on 6 May 1954, run a mile at Oxford in 3m. 59.4s. But even this statement has one or two problems related to its factuality. One criticism that a pedantic revisionist could make is that the time he took was not 3m. 59.4s, simply because it is not theoretically possible to stop time. Taking this tendency towards pedantry a bit further I could argue that with electronic timing, it might have been slightly slower (though not slow enough to make it more than four minutes!). But I will not be following this kind of approach in the pages that follow.

In my first paragraph I was careful *not* to state that Bannister's result was the first time that anyone had broken the 'barrier' of the four-minute mile (I said he was *recorded* as having been the first). A number of stories from north America allude to runners who, before Bannister, were said to have run under four minutes for the mile. It has been suggested, for example, that the former world record holder, Glenn Cunningham had done it alone in practice. Consider, however, a British claim. In June 1987, a Hampstead doctor, John Etheridge, a former secretary of the United Hospitals Athletic Club, international steeplechaser, honorary medical officer of the AAA, and acquaintance – but no friend – of Jack Lovelock, had a letter published in the highly reputable *British Medical Journal* (*BMJ*). In response to a review in the *BMJ* of a biographical novel on Lovelock by the New Zealand author, James McNeish, Etheridge claimed that Lovelock twice ran a sub-four-minute mile in the mid-1930s. These were said to have been performed secretly at Paddington in London and at Motspur Park in Surrey. Etheridge added that he had timed these solo runs and meticulously recorded their details – including the exact distances run and the reliability of the stopwatch – in his diaries. Although, without his notes, he could not recall the precise times Lovelock was supposed to have achieved, he seemed to recall that the Paddington run was done in 3m. 56s and that the time achieved at Motspur Park was 3m. 52.2s, unpaced. Each of these times, if true, would have improved hugely on the world record at the time – the latter by over 80 yards. Etheridge died before his alleged detailed notes could be located. That's all the hard evidence we have – a letter to a journal (and it is always possible that Dr Etheridge was trying to out-do McNeish in the art of 'factional' writing).

If I wanted to *deny* the claim that Bannister was the first four-minute miler, Etheridge's letter is the sort of thing I would use as my 'proof'.

However, I prefer to believe that Bannister was the first because his time was run in public and, even if it wasn't precisely 3m. 59.4s, I am happy to accept that it was close enough to be under four minutes. Many 'facts' are what we are happy to believe – facts tend to be beliefs. The story of Roger Bannister exemplifies the delicate distinction between myth and history.

I am more interested in *interpretation* than in facts. Interpretation is the attempt to give meaning to something or somebody. I do not accumulate (m)any new facts but instead try to re-interpret them. I am particularly interested in reinterpreting Bannister as a 'gentleman amateur' and a 'hero', and all the connotations that these terms carry, one of which being that Bannister was a sort of pre-modern runner, a runner who was out of place in the modern, post-war world of sports. I therefore need to be able to define 'gentleman amateur' (see Chapter 6) since this is what I am suggesting Bannister was not. I also want to suggest that the four-minute mile was not as significant, and not so far from previous performances, as is sometimes thought. Nor might it be as worthy as it was seen at the time.

But there are problems with this approach. I may have prejudices against Bannister, based, for example, on his relatively privileged background compared with my own. To be honest, he was never a teenage hero of mine. My awe was reserved for one of his contemporaries, Gordon Pirie, a world record holder at 5,000 metres, a three-times Olympian, and silver medal winner at the Melbourne Games of 1956. With the passing of time, however, I have gradually rejected my former polarised perceptions of these two athletes. A youthful (perhaps infantile) view has been replaced by one that sees both of them (though in different ways) as thoroughly modern athletes – each of them putting their bodies through painful tests, like everyone else having strengths and weaknesses – human beings *in extremis*.

It is not only my former fannishness that I bring to this book. I have a background as a (former) club-level runner, which means that, to some extent, I can identify with the protocols of running and racing. I was also trained as a geographer, to explore things and people to see if they are in or out of place – literally and metaphorically.

But back to the question of amateurism: if I discover one snippet of information which clearly and unambiguously shows that Roger Bannister was not an amateur, that does not mean to say I have proved that Bannister was not an amateur most of the time. If a single piece of evidence suggests he was not an amateur, it does not mean that all evidence does so. I use this simply as an illustration. In fact, words like 'amateur' are ambiguous and do not carry any single meaning. As his amateur-ness is thought to be one of the qualities that contributed to his heroic status it follows that claims that he was not all that 'amateurish' reflect on his heroism.

In the chapters that follow I want to study Bannister's running career through the words written both by him and about him. These writings – memoirs, biographies, academic tomes, scholarly papers, transcripts of interviews, websites, newspaper and magazine articles – are major contributions to his image as a hero. I am writing about the *representations* of Bannister rather than the man himself, who I can never really know. By 'excavating' such writing, 'layers of truth' can be exposed. This approach is elegantly described by Norman Denzin:

> Lives and their experiences are represented as stories. They are like pictures that have been painted over, and, when paint is scraped off an old picture, something new becomes visible. What is new is what was previously covered up. ... Something new is always coming into sight, displacing what was previously certain and seen. There is no truth in the painting of a life, only multiple images and traces of what has been, what could have been, and what is now.

For example, and a trivial one at that, a recent book on the post-war history of British sport led me to believe that when Bannister ran 3m. 59.4s, he was an Oxford undergraduate. This was my first layer of truth. I then read his autobiography and discovered that he had graduated several years earlier. This provided me with a second layer of truth. I proceeded further and found that he was not even an Oxford student at the time of his famous race; a third layer of truth was exhumed. It is a bit more difficult to question whether he was a 'gentleman amateur', conquering an apparently insurmountable barrier. This is because 'gentleman amateur' is not so precise a term as 'undergraduate'. Even so, I think I am able to interrogate the term 'amateur' and its connotations and in so doing strip away one surface layer of truth, exposing another.

Layers of truth can also be excavated by comparing the writings of the object of this book, Roger Bannister, with the writings of those who have written about him. It should not be assumed, because Roger Bannister wrote an autobiography (or memoir), First Four Minutes, that his words are transparent. Indeed, although his writing informs this book, there are contradictions and opacity in the sentences that Bannister penned. The re-presentation of a life is not the same as that life, and never can be.

In order to arrive at my conclusions I have to describe, in a fair amount of detail, the kind of sporting environment Bannister was operating in. This requires some insights into the history of the world mile record and how these records were achieved. Likewise, I look at some of the events that led Bannister, inexorably or not, towards the races that contributed to his status as 'hero'. The final part of the book examines the aftermath of 6 May 1954 and whether Roger Bannister was in or out of place in the world of modern sports.

There is one final introductory question to be asked and answered. Did I consult Sir Roger Bannister in the writing of this book? The answer is no. I seriously considered contacting him but decided otherwise on the basis of Michael Crick's comments in his stunning biography of another (sort of) Oxford athlete, Jeffrey Archer. Crick argued that the ideal relationship between a biographer (which I am not) and a living subject is 'no direct help, but no obstacles either'. The danger of getting too close can create a sense of obligation and it seems unfair for the object of a study to spend a good deal of time helping an author when the latter succumbs to dwelling too much on the more unfortunate aspects of a life. In any case, as Vladimir Nabokov reminds budding biographers in *The Real Life of Sebastian Knight*, 'Don't be too certain of learning the past from the lips of the present. Beware of the most honest broker'. What one is told is 'shaped by the teller, reshaped by the listener'.

Reading this short book should provide younger readers with some new 'facts'. For those who were around at the time of the four-minute mile it might bring on a burst of nostalgia. For both groups of readers, however, I hope that what follows will enable them to think about a significant moment in Britain's sporting past and perhaps even re-evaluate it.

2

REACHING FOR RECORDS

The kind of running that made Roger Bannister famous is one that generates records – not records as in photography, painting, poetry, biographies and statues but records as in numbers and statistics. The quantified record provides credibility, spurious though it might be. Record mania in athletics has existed since the middle of the nineteenth century. The sage Montague Shearman, former Oxford University sprinter, founder member of the AAA, lawyer, writer and trainer of athletics and football in the 1880s, felt that it had all gone too far. Articulated in the language of the protestant reformation, he believed that 'the worshipping of records is idolatrous, and inconsistent with the true sportsman'. He 'could see no reason for placing the acquisition of a "record" as the summit of an athlete's ambition' because having covered a given distance faster than anyone else did not prove that the runner concerned was the better athlete.

Shearman also recognised that the statistics that litter record books and ranking lists are presented totally out of context. Does a four-minute mile run by a well-trained athlete mean the same thing as one run by a total novice? Is a result achieved in wind and pouring rain on a muddy track worth the same as an identical time run in perfect conditions? Shearman was supported half-a-century later by the sporting brothers, Adolphe and Harold Abrahams. They stated that as 'an absolute index of the actual capacity of individual runners, time records are of little or no value'. Results, therefore, are relatively good or relatively bad, relatively fast or relatively slow. However, the power of statistics has prevailed and the public and the athletes prefer numbers to words. 3m. 59.4s means more than 'a good run'. The simulation (the bare statistic) means more than the reality (a visceral, indescribable experience).

MAKING AND BREAKING RECORDS

To make a record there is a requirement that speed is increased. Speed is one of the essences of the modern world, arguably the essence of sports like foot-racing. There are no style prizes so looking elegant is incidental, unless elegance increases efficiency. Aesthetics have to make way for scientific measurement. The general history of racing has been dominated by an increase in speed, in acceleration. How is speed increased over time? By more people taking part in serious sports, by the use of more intensive methods of training and by the application of science and technology: lighter shoes, faster tracks, better diet, the use of amphetamines and steroids. But in such cases, who makes and owns the record? Can it really be the athlete alone? Does the shoemaker have a stake in it? The coach? The chemist? And who owns the runner's body? I make this vaguely philosophical diversion because it will come to bear on the life of the alleged 'gentleman amateur', Roger Bannister.

Records are like an appetite and encourage excess. We always want more – and the more we want them the more we are willing to go to extreme means to achieve them. A record will always be broken and like the horizon, once it is reached, another appears. This is where the parallel of the four-minute mile with the climbing of Everest stops. While only one person can be the first to achieve either, there is an important difference between climbing the highest mountain in the world and the breaking of the four-minute barrier. Nobody could ever climb higher than Hillary and Tenzing; there were hundreds who could, and would, break Bannister's record. It has become commonplace. Bannister is renowned for being the first – and he wanted it that way. For him it was much more than breaking a record: it was breaking a barrier, an arbitrary and imaginary barrier but, for most people and some athletes, a barrier nevertheless.

The possibility of the four-minute mile was being mooted well before Bannister was born but some pundits, even in the 1930s, still felt it was impossible. In 1935, for example, Brutus Hamilton, a well-known coach at the University of California, felt, with statistical certainty, that the limit of human achievement was a mile in exactly 4m. 1.66s! At the time of baby Bannister's birth in 1929, the record stood at 4m. 10.4s, set by the 'flying Finn' from Turku, Paavo Nurmi (Figure 2.1), in 1923. Nurmi was also nicknamed 'the running machine' and often raced with a stopwatch in his hand, eliminating the human element. This feature – a machine attached to a man – was highly symbolic in the history of the mile race. He used the watch as a pacemaker. In scientific parlance a pacemaker is a device for controlling or influencing rhythmic activity. The machine was to control the athlete, to dictate the correct pace. The search for the right pace, and the right pacemaker, are central to the history of the quest for the four-minute mile.

Nurmi was one of a large number of Finns who revolutionised middle-distance running in the inter-war years. His countryman, Hannes Kolehmainen, who had won the Olympic 5,000 and 10,000 metres at the 1912 Stockholm Olympics, had inspired him. With a good dose of hyperbole, Kolehmainen was said to have run Finland on to the world map. The training adopted by the mainly working-class Finns surpassed what most other runners had regarded as normal. Kolehmainen was said to have turned running into a science, this – and the alleged qualities of the physical environment of the northern lands – being thought to be the basis of the Finns' masterful performances. But the top athletes

Figure 2.1 Paavo Nurmi (author's photograph)

in the newly independent country worked part-time and received financial aid from various sources ('expenses' and payment from gate receipts). Running was, more or less, their job. It paid off and they dominated the Olympics during the 1920s and 1930s.

Nurmi, in particular, was dedicated to running, as exact in his athletics as he was to be in the building business he set up following his retirement from the track. At his peak he trained three to four hours daily. His training included walking, running and calisthenics. On 20 occasions he broke world records, adopting scientific principles of training (Nurmi was educated in running from a book by the British runner, Alfred Shrubb, and his best subject at the technical college in Turku was mathematics). He maintained meticulous records of his training, his *leitmotif* being planning, persistence and pacing. He believed the fastest time that could ever be achieved for the mile was 4m. 4s. In a word, Nurmi was the first modern runner and modernised the world of track running.

In 1923 Nurmi set his world mile record of 4m. 10.4s at the beautiful Stockholm Olympic Stadium, with its 385 metres track, built for the 1912 Games. A 'race' was arranged in which he had only one opponent, Edvin Wide from Sweden, a world-class athlete himself, who led for the fast first lap in 58.5s. A slower first lap, it was argued, might have led him to achieve his aim of recording 4m. 8s. But this one-on-one race, with two runners in a record attempt, was rational enough since no 'also-rans' were around to clutter up the track and distract attention. This kind of arrangement was typical of Nurmi's other record-breaking runs: 'He reserved his record-setting for small competitions organised specifically for the purpose' – a description that I will show fitted perfectly the subject of this book. Nurmi had broken a record (4m. 12.6s by the American, Norman Taber) that G.P. Meade had described as 'an almost superhuman feat' – indeed, the ultimate performance. It 'taxed the imagination' that anyone could cut five seconds, let alone ten, off this stupendous result.

Nurmi became an international icon. He raced all over Europe: Stockholm, Berlin, London (Stamford Bridge), Paris, Antwerp, Vienna, Warsaw. He was a man in demand. His appeal stretched across the Atlantic and he competed indoors at Madison Square Garden, New York, and outdoors at the Los Angeles Coliseum. San Francisco, Chicago, Boston, Detroit, Toronto, Montreal and Ottawa were only some of the other American venues on his 1925 itinerary. He rubbed shoulders with film stars but shunned celebrity, favouring training and racing. He made a lot of money, notably satisfying the demands of American and German promoters in return for cash payments, but was exposed and then banned, shortly before the 1932 Los Angeles Olympics in which he was to run the marathon. He had infringed what for many was the basic protocol of amateur running; he had run for money in exchange for performing his skills, winning races or breaking records. Known to be tight-fisted, 'first money, then running' was what he demanded of event promoters. He was no mere amateur (in any sense of the word) but a serious runner who took training methods into realms previously unknown.

At the same time, he was described as a neurotic. Martti Jukola, a famous Finnish sports journalist, wrote in 1935: 'There was something inhumanly stern and cruel about him, but he conquered the world by pure means: with a will that had supernatural power'. But was he, like other runners before and after him, cruel to himself? A French writer said of him: 'Athletics is the only king he acknowledges, the only god he serves to whom he has consecrated all his sacrifices, his pain, his suffering, his soul and his life. But nobody knows if he gets any pleasure out of it'.

Despite the predictions of permanence, Nurmi's record lasted only eight years. Perhaps, like the four-minute mile, 4m. 10s was a kind of psychological barrier. But, inevitably, it was broken. In 1931, Frenchman Jules Ladoumègue, in a planned record attempt, including a pacemaker who led for half-a-mile, clocked 4m. 9.2s at the Stade Jean Bouin in Paris. With the 4m. 10s barrier broken, the four-minute mile appeared dimly visible on the horizon of the record.

The world record for the mile was steadily eroded. During the 1930s no dramatic improvements took place but records did not last long. Records were broken, not smashed. In 1933 the New Zealander and Oxford student, Jack Lovelock chipped it down to 4m. 7.6s in an exciting race with Bill Bronthon of the USA in the Princeton University Stadium, New Jersey. Lovelock who, like Nurmi, sometimes carried a stopwatch while racing, was gripped and fascinated by a scientific approach to running. Even so, a year earlier at the Iffley Road track in Oxford, with its three laps to the mile circuit and with a nine feet drop at one end, he had run 4m. 12s. His pace was as uneven as the track, though this performance could, of course, have been an 'experiment'. His respective quarter-mile times were 57s, 65s, 71s, and 59s. The famous coach, 'Sam' Mussabini, was amazed, suggesting that 'if he could only have run to one of my even-timed schedules, he might have got the four-minute mile'.

Lovelock's record was beaten by the barrel-chested American, Glenn Cunningham (known as the 'Iron Horse of Kansas'), again in the Princeton Stadium, a year later with a time of 4m. 6.7s (the International Amateur Athletics Federation [IAAF] liked to keep records to the nearest fifth of a second so the time was rounded up to 4m. 6.8s. So if anyone ran 3m. 59.9s it would be officially recognised as 4 minutes). Cunningham was a product of the US college sports set-up. He was a 'student-athlete', a category that stretched to the limits the concept of the amateur athlete. To an extent, such athletic recruits were paid to run, receiving as they did athletics scholarships, euphemistically described as 'grants in aid'.

Cunningham's record lasted for three years. It was broken by the British runner, Sydney Wooderson (Figure 2.2) in circumstances that reflect a bygone age. In Britain, a popular form of running in the 1930s was handicap racing in which each runner started the race at varying distances from scratch, or the starting line. This caused a lot of bodies to be littered around the track but if the runners were judiciously chosen, a good race – and pace – could ensue. Top-class runners, including Wooderson, were not averse to taking part in handicap races.

During the 1930s, Wooderson was the top runner in Britain. He was a bespectacled Blackheath Harrier whose physical appearance was the polar opposite of that of the Kansas 'Iron Horse'. Wooderson did not fit the athletic stereotype, being short and frail-looking and having poor eyesight. His black running outfit contributed to a somewhat quaint, Victorian image. Privately educated but trained as a solicitor rather than a scholar, Wooderson had been threatening to beat the world's best for a couple of years. Tipped to challenge for the 1936 Olympic title, he was injured during the Games and failed to qualify

Figure 2.2 Sydney Wooderson (author's collection)

for the final. By 1937, however, he had regained a supreme level of fitness and at the London University track at Motspur Park he was entered for a mile handicap event, starting, of course, from scratch. The British international, Reginald Thomas was given the role of pacemaker, off ten yards, and led Wooderson through the half-mile. Ahead of him ran other runners who acted as targets, one being Wooderson's brother, Stanley. Getting to three-quarters of a mile in 3m. 7.2s he sprinted a sub-59s last lap to record 4m. 6.4s, just failing to catch his brother off a big handicap. Sydney Wooderson had become the first British world record holder for the mile since the IAAF became the sport's governing bureaucracy in 1912. It was thought he could run even faster and the 1920 Olympic gold medallist, Albert Hill, thought that the little Londoner was capable of running the mile in 4m. 3s.

WARTIME, WOODERSON AND AFTER

Wooderson's training methods were very different from those who were to follow him into the record books. In the autumn and spring he would run on the road and grass, at a steady pace and covering three to five miles. At weekends he would do lots of walking. As the summer approached he would train almost daily, mainly on the track, and include a good deal of fast running. Brisk walking was also a popular form of training at the time. It could not really be described as a 'system' but it suited him.

Wooderson's career as a top-class runner continued into the 1940s and, in due course, he was to lower his best mile time. But the Second World War was to intervene. He carried on running, unfit for active service because of his relatively poor eyesight. During the war he ran races that attracted huge crowds. Over 50,000 watched him win the inelegantly named 'The Stalin Mile' in Manchester in 1944, for example. The proceeds went to the war effort. The times he recorded in wartime were normally around 4m. 11s, good enough to beat the best that Britain could offer. But there was no serious competition to nudge him towards more records.

While Wooderson was running in British wartime, things in neutral Sweden were dramatically different. Throughout the war two Swedish runners, Gunder Hägg and Arne Andersson (Figure 2.3), traded the world mile record between them. A regular racing programme continued to flourish, with foreigners, including Germans, taking part in some of the competitions. In the early 1940s Hägg also competed in Germany. With his compatriots he was attracted to a system of training that may have contributed to their success. Steady running on roads

Figure 2.3 Gunder Hägg leading Arne Andersson (author's collection)

and occasional running on the track had been replaced by a method introduced in Germany known as 'interval running' where running over a specified distance (say 400 metres) was repeated many times with a short recovery period between each run (see later). The Swedish modification of interval running was to shift it from the geometrically defined running track and take it to the Swedish forests, meadows and lakeland beaches. Here the athletes would train in a rural idyll. Sprinting, striding and resting, they would be refreshed by an ever-changing nature, not constrained by the sterility of the stadium. They would learn from the rural, from the Swedish soil. This method was termed 'speed-play' or, in Swedish, *fartlek*, and was to be adopted by many runners worldwide. Roger Bannister would be one of them.

At 8 p.m. on 1 July 1942, Hägg and Andersson lined up for a mile race at the tree-girt Slottskogsvallen track in the western Swedish seaport of Gothenburg. Two pacemakers were readily available. One led the first lap and the other got the two stars to the half-mile in just over two minutes, at which point Hägg and Andersson took over with Hägg finishing in 4m. 6.2s, a fifth of a second inside Wooderson's time. Andersson was close behind, equalling it.

Having reported the feats of the two Swedes, Harold Abrahams, the former Olympic sprint champion, lawyer, athletics journalist and doyen of British diggers-up and compilers of athletics statistics, speculated that because it had taken five years to reduce Wooderson's record by a fifth of a second, it would take 150 years to reach four minutes. His extrapolation, based only on one period between the two records, was flawed but, at the same time, showed that talk of the four-minute mile would not go away. Had he waited just a little longer, he would have had to significantly adjust his prognostication. Only nine days after Hägg's record, Andersson, who earlier in the year had won a 1,500 metres race against a relay team made up of 15 schoolboy runners, each running a 100 metres stint, turned up for another mile in the 1912 red-brick and granite built, gothic Olympic Stadium in Stockholm. There was no holding him. In a solo performance he ran all the way from the front to equal Hägg's time, a spectacular run in which the second athlete finished ten seconds (about 80 yards) behind.

In early September 1942 Hägg ran another mile. The venue was Stockholm. On this occasion, the pacemaker ran the first quarter-mile in the very fast time of 56s with Hägg ten metres behind, but by halfway he was ahead. The fast first lap was compensated for by two slower middle laps but he still finished in a world record time – 4m. 4.6s. The world record had been broken three times in one year. The speedy Swedes refused to let up. In 1943 it was again Andersson's turn. In an astonishing race in Gothenburg he took on the best of the other Swedes, excluding Hägg but featuring an up-and-coming runner, Lennart Strand. The pacemaker was Arne Ahlsén who led for three-quarters of a mile (leading the field, not just Andersson) with a time of 3m. 3.5s. Andersson upped the pace followed a few yards behind by a coterie of Swedish milers but prevailed over them by about 12 metres to win in yet another world record time of 4m. 2.6s. In third place was the pacemaker who ran 4m. 6.6s. Such was the depth of Swedish 'miling'. How much longer could this go on?

The following year Hägg broke the world 1,500 metres record with a time of 3m. 43s. This was regarded by track and field statisticians as the metric equivalent of four minutes for the mile. However, Andersson confirmed his status as the best Swedish miler when, at the southern port city of Malmö, he faced Hägg again over the 'English mile'. The four-minute mile was now less than one second per lap faster than the world record. Five runners lined up for the start. Strand took the first lap, Hägg led by the end of the second and Andersson at the bell in 2m. 59.6s. They were less than a minute away from four minutes. A great race ensued but Andersson's last lap took 62s, just fast enough to out-sprint Hägg in yet another world record time of 4m. 1.6s. The latter also broke the old record with 4m. 2s.

'Gunder the wonder', as he was dubbed, toured the USA in much the same way that Nurmi had done. He was more than a miler and by the end of his career he had held world records in six different track events, metric and imperial. While in America he mixed with film stars and met his favourite, Greer Garson. But even a fairly hectic social schedule did not prevent him from carrying out his daily training, in fields and woodlands away from the city streets.

SETTING THE TARGET

The war ended in 1945. The record-breaking did not. On 15 July the usual names gathered for a mile race in Malmö – Andersson, Hägg, Strand and Rune Persson. A pacemaker led through the first lap in 56.2s with Hägg on his heels. At halfway Hägg led, the clock showing 1m. 58.5s, and he continued to lead to the finish. Andersson was below par, the result of having impaled on his spikes a spent cartridge shell that a careless starter had left on the track. Hägg's time was 4m. 1.3s (rounded up to an official time of 4m. 1.4s), yet again, a new world record. And he seemed to have plenty in reserve as he crossed the line, showing no signs of distress and readily undertaking a lap of honour. Following the race he declared that the four-minute mile could no longer be seen as a problem. 'I believe I could have done it today had there been more competition', he remarked. So might Andersson, had it not been for his unusual mishap. Nevertheless, it was Hägg's record, as much as the four-minute mile, that became the barrier to beat. It would remain intact until May 1954.

The end of hostilities permitted renewed contact between British athletes and those from the rest of Europe. Sydney Wooderson, who was still running and who looked forward to competing against the Swedes, had been suffering from rheumatic fever but by the summer of 1945 he was getting fit, though hardly ready to take on the world record holder, Hägg or, for that matter, Andersson. However, the British August Bank Holiday traditionally featured a big athletics meeting at London's White City Stadium in Shepherd's Bush. It had been built for the 1908 Olympics and was now owned by the Greyhound Racing Association, which meant that there was quite a distance between the athletes and the spectators, the greyhound track being outside the running track. Nevertheless, this was the first big athletics event since the end of the war and the gates had to be closed with about 57,000 people packed inside.

Among them was Ralph Bannister who had travelled down from Harrow with his 16-year-old son, Roger. It was his first view of the real world of sport, serious running on a proper track, a huge crowd and overseas competitors. As a young, impressionable, teenager he seemed to revel in it, happy to stand for four hours. The only top-class athlete he had seen previously was the British international miler, Doug Wilson, who he once watched running a three-quarter mile time-trial at a dusty, black running track, set among trees in a municipal park in Wealdstone, near where he lived. Bannister was in awe, seeing Wilson as a superman. But what he was to witness at the White City Stadium was more than awesome; it was inspiring.

The main crowd pullers were Wooderson and the two record breakers from Sweden, Hägg and Andersson. Hägg ran the two miles, winning easily. But the main event was the mile – a contest between Andersson and Wooderson. The event was full of symbolism: the Adonis-like visitor from well-fed Sweden facing Wooderson, the 'deprived', waif-like Briton living on rationed food. In fact, there was little doubt about who would win. Andersson led for almost the entire distance, coming home in, for him, the slow time of 4m. 8.8s with 'our Sydney' close behind. For Wooderson it was a remarkable run, something that had not been lost on the boy Bannister. Rather than the Nordic blond, it was Wooderson, the slight, five feet six inches, dark-haired, balding, bespectacled, clerical-looking underdog who looked like he needed improving, who became his sports hero, admired as much for his attitudes as for his achievements on the track. Sixteen is an impressionable age and Bannister claimed that seeing Wooderson was the defining moment in his running career, something that inspired him with a new interest.

Wooderson's contact with the Swedish opposition did not end with this defeat. A month after the White City race he had a re-match against Andersson, this time in Gothenburg. The month's training had given Wooderson strength and speed to get back to his mid-1930s form, showing that his continuous training during the war had been beneficial. The race had been arranged with typical Swedish efficiency: 1,500 metre times would be taken and, as usual, a pacemaker was readily available. A local runner took the field through the half-mile in just outside two minutes. A four-minute mile looked possible but Andersson slowed the pace slightly with the 30-year-old Briton staying with him. With a furlong (220 yards) left to run, Wooderson took the lead and sped through the 1,500 meters point, where he broke a separate tape that had been erected, in a new British record of 3m. 48.4s. He carried on sprinting and was still in the lead with 50 yards to go. Andersson's superior fitness prevailed and he crossed the finishing line in 4m. 3.4s. Wooderson, just behind, recorded a new British mile record of 4m. 4.2s. This was the time that British milers would have to beat before setting their targets at four minutes. Just over a year later Roger Bannister entered Oxford University.

Hägg and Andersson may not have fulfilled their potential. The Swedish sports federation discovered that they were not operating under the amateur rules and had been taking money beyond their expenses. In the social democracies of northern Europe, people were looked after, from pacemakers to winners. The two record breakers were effectively banned from further competition. As with Nurmi, the rules had been written for a previous age, an age where things were not taken too seriously, when you could afford to be an amateur, in the sense that you were not paid for running.

The demise of the two giants of European middle-distance running made space for a new Nordic hero, Lennart Strand. He won the European 1,500 metres title in 1946 and in the same year made an attack on the world record for that distance. The race was in Malmö. He was in the form of his life and managed to equal Hägg's record of 3m. 43s, finishing full of running and in no way appearing distressed. This led him to claim that he had felt sufficiently fresh to have covered the extra 119 yards in the 17 seconds left for a four-minute mile. This was a plausible claim as Andersson had covered this last stretch in 15.2s and both Hägg and Wooderson had done it in under 16s. The caveat is that in none of these races was the 1,500 metres mark reached in less than 3m. 45s. Even so, Strand's run resulted in the four-minute mile being hot gossip. In more ways than one, it was only a matter of time.

What emerges from this brief review of miling from the 1920s to the late 1940s is that it was a serious, scientific, record-breaking business. And it was, like other businesses, one in which money changed hands. It was professional, if not in name. It was also a time when runners sought to find every means of taking an advantage over each other. Once upon a time, the notion of training may have been stigmatised as being 'unfair'. I can imagine a defeated runner complaining that he was beaten because his victor had been training, hence giving him an advantage. Once training became acceptable, one athlete may have been advantaged over another by better training methods, a better coach, better equipment, payment, better pills and tablets, better amphetamines and (later) steroids – and so on. Lovelock, for example, was a loner who was dedicated to proving that he was the greatest athlete the world had ever seen, experimenting on himself in all sorts of ways, both with physiological tests and drugs.

In the 1920s the sports authorities in Germany thought it necessary to warn athletes of the danger of 'doping' though a British view at the time, from the brothers Abrahams, had a familiar ring: 'We have never heard of an athlete utilising dangerous drugs'. A record may have become an ex-record because the world had moved on from an 'amateur' approach. The two decades from 1920 to 1940 illustrated this perfectly and even in England, where the 'gentleman amateur' ethos had arguably reached its peak in the 1920s, it was being undermined by the 1930s. There was no shortage of English-published books on running that adopted a modern, 'scientific' perspective. In the 1930s Arthur Newton, F.A.M. Webster and the Abrahams brothers were among a number of writers who advanced a scientific approach to training. For middle-distance runners 'who intend to enter open competitions' Newton advocated 'continuous daily practice'.

Additionally, I have shown that during this period, world mile records were almost always set with the aid of a pacemaker. The Swedes and Wooderson used pacemakers in different forms, but pacemakers they were. This was a very well-established part of the sport, and had been so in England since the nineteenth century. Montague Shearman loathed this practice. He observed that when an athlete used a pacemaker to break a record, he has everything to win and nothing to lose; no pluck nor skill would be needed to defeat his 'competitors', since none would be of the same standard as him. What he admired were competitions between 'equally matched antagonists'. I quote Shearman here because he can be regarded as a good example of those Victorians who wished to uphold 'sportsmanship' and the amateur ideals of yesteryear. But he was not the only critic. Some years later the Abrahams brothers, in their *Training for Athletics*, devoted over four pages to the practice of pacemaking. They recognised that 'legitimate pacemaking' could easily degenerate into 'track tactics' which they found objectionable. They much preferred 'direct competition'. Totally alien to these critics would have been a star runner with no serious competition, with a pacemaker thrown in. On the other hand, Mussabini claimed that the benefits of being shielded 'from direct air pressure … may be reasonably estimated to equal about 25 yeards in a mile, or around 4 to 5 seconds in time equivalent'.

A further point to bear in mind is that before, but especially during, the period of Swedish domination of the world mile record, world record-breaking races usually had a very small number of competitors, few of whom had a serious chance of winning. This meant that, with a pacemaker at work, the field would soon be strung out, each runner 'knowing his place', the only record they could hope for being a personal one.

Looking back on those fantastic years of the 1940s it might be asked why the Swedes broke records but never shattered them, why they chipped away the decimal places but neither broke the previous record by seconds, nor got below four minutes. One reason might be the way in which speed was distributed over the four quarters of the mile. Three broad theories of pace existed. The first was that the runner should more or less rest during the first half of the race and at that point go flat out to the finish. This was based on the assumption that the athletes would be under strain for a relatively small fraction of the overall race. This was a strategy used by the aforementioned Cunningham of the USA. The British coach, soldier, javelin champion, *News of the World* reporter and prolific writer of training manuals, F.A.M. Webster, felt that this might well be the way to achieve the four-minute mile.

The second model was practised by Nurmi and advocated during the 1920s and 1930s by the British physiologist Archibald Vivian Hill, himself a runner with best times of 53s for the 440 yards and 4m. 45s for the mile. He felt that the best distribution of speed was to spread it evenly during the duration of a race. It was important not to wear oneself out in the early stages and to leave something in hand for the finishing straight. The main problem with this approach, it was thought, was the maintenance of the same speed during the third lap.

The third possibility was that there should be a fast start on the assumption that when the runner is fresh he wouldn't feel any extra effort when going faster on the first lap. Whether intended or not, this was the pattern found among some of the Swedish records set by Andersson and Hägg. In these, the quarter-mile, undertaken by the ubiquitous pacemaker, was often extremely fast. First laps of 56s or 57s were common in half-mile events but in a mile such a fast pace builds up a burden of fatigue that could end in pain, exhaustion and collapse.

The Swedes may have subscribed to the third approach; they may not have fully digested Hill's message or they may have suffered from obsessive bravado. Who is to say that the four-minute mile would not have been broken in the mid-1940s if the pacemaking had been more efficient and that a more even pace had been imposed?

3

FOUNDATIONS OF THE FOUR-MINUTE MILE

In the mid-1950s it was emphatically stated by the medical scientist, Adolphe Abrahams, that 'the athlete who regards his indulgence as a pastime cannot be expected to compete successfully against one who by inclination and circumstances is able to make it the whole business of his life'. At about the same time the renowned track coach at the University of Pennsylvania, Ken Doherty, observed that 'professionalism had taken a stranglehold on distance running'. Serious running was a serious business. By the 1950s there was no room for the hobbyist runner in the world of serious sport.

This was the context into which Roger Bannister's career as a runner fitted neatly. The professionalism of 'amateur' running had been graphically illustrated by the exploits of Kolehmainen and Nurmi in the 1920s and Hägg and Andersson in the 1940s. Their approaches were adapted by Americans and other western European runners in the decade that followed. They were modern, planned, methodical, scientific and professional.

RUNNING AT SCHOOL AND COLLEGE

Writing about his early years Bannister said: 'Usually I played alone'; he lived in a world of his own and at the age of eight he was 'shy, timid and easily frightened'. At school he disliked feeling out of place – a Londoner out of place in Bath – a bit of a loner, occasionally the butt of bullies. He disliked the institutional nature of school where he found that individualism was stifled. He remarked that his teachers 'were always trying to make a man out of me', implying a somewhat feminine side to his personality. However, it could not be said that he disliked learning. On the contrary, he voraciously accumulated knowledge from diverse fields. But it seems that he preferred the freedom to learn than the constraint of being taught:

> I realised ... how delicately one's individual freedom is poised. Though most of us were perhaps unaware of it, the school was in fact governed more by fear in one way or another, than by respect and tolerance. This made compromises difficult either with other boys or with the masters. Under these conditions freedom to explore and expand was always in danger.

Questions of individual freedom and compromise were to feature frequently in his running career.

Bannister did some running at school. It suited him. He was not attracted to rugby football, his temperament and his slim build seemingly more appropriate for striding than to scrummage. He displayed a good turn of speed and 'given the choice between a solitary run and a series of meaningless and for [him] difficult exercises in the gym, [he] always chose the run'. Through running, he was able to continue an individualistic kind of life (as a 'misfit' with 'an inferiority complex', as he put it) but at the same time not feel totally isolated. More than once, his speed helped him put distance between himself and those who teased or threatened him. Indeed, his running could provide the prestige that he was unable to find in rugby and boxing. When it came to racing, he ran to exhaustion.

The kind of schools he attended placed a certain amount of faith in cross-country running, a somewhat sadistic practice born of the Victorian desire to use running over fields and through mud and streams as a form of social control. The worst of its excesses are well documented in *Tom Brown's Schooldays*. While in Bath, Bannister won the school cross-country race a year earlier than was expected but he did not take it too seriously. His so-called training simply involved running flat out for two miles or so, feeling totally exhausted at the end. This was hardly the scientised training that he would later pick up at Oxford and might be better referred to as common sense training, an approach suited to the 'gentleman amateur' that would not create too much of a disjuncture with daily life. Over-training was to be avoided, suggesting a consistency with late nineteenth-century scientific thinking. But having said that, it was not based on techniques that depended on research *specifically directed at* understanding the physiological processes that would enhance athletic performance.

The genealogy of Bannister's early running has been further augmented by information recorded by Harold Abrahams. In the long-defunct monthly magazine, *World Sports*, he claimed that at the age of '11 or so' Bannister ran the half-mile in 2m. 30s and at University College School he lowered this time to 2m. 15s. This was a modest, but far from hopeless, time for a 15- or 16-year-old sixth-form runner. He also did some rowing (arguably an even more exhausting activity than cross-country running) and on attending Oxford at the age of 17 he had a penchant for it. A Corinthian might have run *and* rowed but the days of the non-specialist were long over. The Abrahams brothers had deplored the cult of the *victor ludorum* in the 1920s and advocated specialisation. In his book, *Running*, Arthur Newton had stressed that 'specialisation nowadays is a necessity'. At Cambridge, Adolphe and Harold Abrahams had, on many occasions, witnessed young men who had won everything from the 100 yards to the mile at school but had ultimately failed 'to gain even a half-blue at the 'Varsity'. The modern model of sport existed at Oxbridge despite suggestions to the contrary and the image of Wooderson and his plucky run at the White City Stadium prevailed over that of the 'Boat Race'. Bannister became a runner.

At Oxford, Bannister's college was Exeter (Figure 3.1), founded in 1314, in the centre of town, tucked away in Turl Street but also facing on to 'the Broad', across the road from Blackwell's bookshop. It was also accessible to both the University Parks and Christchurch Meadow for training. A bicycle ride away, over the river at Iffley Road, was the university running track, three laps to the mile, where athletes ran in a clockwise. Unbeknown to him at the time, Bannister was entering a college that claimed to have formed the first athletics club in the world in 1850. It was also the *alma mater* of the New Zealander Jack Lovelock, as already noted, the 1936 Olympic 1,500 metres champion and former world record holder for, yes, the mile. Even so, one of the English tutors at Exeter, Nevil Coghill (who translated Chaucer into modern English), was also known for his assertion that 'great athletes rarely

Figure 3.1 Exeter College, Oxford (author's photograph)

make great scholars' – a pretty bold statement that Bannister might have pondered.

On arrival at Oxford, Bannister found himself within a stone's throw of the Bodleian Library, the Sheldonian Theatre and the Ashmolean Museum. But these were not his priorities and 'without waiting to admire [his] new college [he] dropped his bags and set off for the running track'. He did not have to wait to be pressed into athletics by his college sports club which might have incurred an ignominious 'debagging' if he refused. Running was where his priorities would lie – for at least a sizeable proportion of his time at university.

Oxford University Athletic Club (OUAC) had a well-structured set-up for sports, well in advance of most other athletic clubs in Britain. Members of the club were privileged, not only by their social background but also because of their access to the sporting facilities and the considerable emphasis placed on sports. They had fixtures and championships at different levels. Newcomers to the university could take part in the Freshmen's Sports soon after their arrival; inter-college sport was very popular; there were well-experienced coaches available, they had their own running track, open spaces in the city for training and famous Oxbridge alumni such as Jack Lovelock or Harold Abrahams who might turn up to inspire and advise. Funded foreign tours – to the USA, Germany and Finland, for example – were far from uncommon. In any case, for most students, money was no problem. Of those at Oxford in the late 1940s about 60 per cent of male students came from the so-called 'public' schools (that were attended by less than ten per cent of the population as a whole) and had well-heeled parents. Additionally, when Bannister arrived, 90 per cent were former national servicemen. Compared with pre-war undergraduates, such men may have been more inclined to take their studies seriously, as preparation for the next stage in their lives. They were always ready with advice for a callow youth.

Bannister arrived in the city of dreaming spires at a time when the emphasis placed on sport was relatively strong. Some colleges liked the idea of having good-looking sportsmen about the place. Athletic competition and the achievement of a 'blue' (that is, having represented the university against Cambridge) still meant something, and in some occupations a 'blue' was worth more than a degree. It was not really until the early 1960s, when grants to students from local education authorities became mandatory, that pressure was applied to eliminate the dilettante athlete who was happy to spend three years engaged in leisurely – or serious – sports. In other words, a budding athlete could no longer get away with doing a minimal amount of academic work. Eventually, a college's performance on the Norrington Table (that compared the quality of each college's academic output) became more important than the results of its sports teams. Not that Roger Bannister would waste time. He would work hard and run hard.

I have already noted that being at Oxford was a privilege. Think of the number of working-class boys who sacrificed a life of running and racing for one of working eight-'til-five in a factory or foundry. Think of the runners who lacked the wealth to attend university and, moreover, could not, in the 1950s, make money from advertising sporting or other goods. Whereas professional cricketers like Denis Compton and Len Hutton could add to their income by advertising 'Brylcreem' and jock straps respectively, the only money international runners could obtain (officially) were paltry expenses. To run at the highest level, they often lost money. Also, recall the lack of facilities for running in many parts of 1950s' Britain. To be sure, some working-class runners did make it in spite of the environment in which they had been reared and today it is recognised that in the 1950s, many top-class British runners often received substantial payments for running, both in Britain and overseas. Indeed, later on it was alumni of Oxford University, men like Chris Chataway and Derek Johnston, who most vociferously argued for a more open system of payments.

A former world record holder for the mile, Derek Ibbotson, recently recalled British athletics in the 1950s with the words, 'nobody [that is, in top-class athletics] was amateur, except for maybe Bannister'. *Maybe*

Bannister was not paid in cash but he certainly acquired fantastic cultural, social and economic advantages, compared with the majority of the nation. An Oxford education; the time he had for training; the sporting facilities and advisers available to him; the cultural capital he was subsequently able to cash in on. Clearly, such privilege is unfair but it is not regarded as cheating. 'Fair play' is said to still exist in such conditions of inequality of opportunity but as inequality (of opportunity, physicality, etc.) will always exist, the notion of 'fair play' is arguably difficult to sustain.

I have to admit, however, that Bannister *was* studying and not skiving while at Oxford. He had always wanted to be a doctor and by 1952 he had obtained a BA and MSc in Physiology, both with the help of scholarships. But to say that Oxbridge athletes could 'not train so lengthily or rigorously' as non-university people (as one academic has written) is the opposite of the truth. Afternoons at Oxford had been given over to 'exercise' since the mid-nineteenth century and only an Oxbridge man could write, as Bannister did, that middle-distance runners could practise with sprinters 'in an afternoon's training'. How could the workingman-athlete possibly train *in the afternoon*? At Oxford, Bannister took full advantage of all that was available. He even listened to the comments of the old Iffley Road groundsman who, with respect, warned him one winter afternoon, that 'I'm afraid you'll never be any good, sir. You just haven't got the strength or the build for it'. He would have to wait and see.

Bannister's first ever mile race was in the Freshmen's and Seniors' sports in October 1946 (Figure 3.2). At that time his training was indeed 'amateurish', little different from that of his schooldays, and he was pleasantly surprised when he finished second behind an older freshman, Peter Curry, who was to run for Britain in the 1948 Olympic steeplechase and become a close friend. Bannister bounded along, like a kangaroo, some said, over-striding, partly because it was the first time he had raced in spikes. His time was nearer five minutes than four – 4m. 53s, one second behind the winner. The raw statistic suggests a

Figure 3.2 Roger Bannister in the lead in his first mile race, Iffley Road, Oxford, 1946. Note the clockwise direction of the runners (*The Oxford Mail*)

modest result; even in the immediate post-war period several British schoolboys could have run faster. On the other hand, it was in October, on a track with a severe incline, and he had only been at the varsity for a matter of weeks. What's more, his time was 15 seconds faster than that of the winner of the Seniors' race. And if he followed the advice of the university coach, given after the race, to stop 'bounding', he could improve his mile time by half-a-minute. A couple of days later, Bannister also had a go at the three miles, again finishing second to Curry, in over 16 minutes.

A month or so later young Bannister found himself in rather different circumstances. He had been initiated to cross-country running at school and, in the English 'harrier' tradition, he continued doing so at Oxford. Unsurprisingly, young Bannister was not deemed good enough for the Oxford first team in the 1946 inter-varsity cross-country race, run over seven-and-a-half miles of rough country at Roehampton Common – a course that required the intrepid crossing of Beverley Brook as well as the negotiation of ploughed fields. However, he managed to finish as runner-up in the second team race. He was also picked for the university to take part in a low-key cross-country race against Blackheath Harriers. At the time his hero, Wooderson, was nearing the end of his career, preparing himself for a specialisation in cross-country. Whether the youthful Oxonian knew it or not is unclear but both Wooderson and Bannister found themselves in the same race. It was a moderate field. Wooderson finished third, Bannister fifth. It was the only time the hero and his acolyte would compete against each other.

Bannister also ran cross-country for a north London club, Finchley Harriers, with whom he hoped to get races during the long university vacation. He ran for them in the Middlesex County cross-country championships over five miles but underestimated the effects of a late night's jollifications and drinking at a Hunt Ball. He still finished ninth in the race. More controversially, however, having joined the local club he had unknowingly denied the Achilles Club (an elite club of Oxbridge athletes nominated by their universities) the right to claim him. Favouring the Oxbridge group he immediately resigned from Finchley. This one race was his only real experience of running for a typical British athletics club.

The 'Oxford system' enabled Bannister to progress considerably and rapidly. Less than six months later, in March 1947, while still in his freshman year, he was named as the third member of the Oxford team for the mile in the annual match against 'the other' university, Cambridge. Whereas two years earlier he had been ogling at the feats of Wooderson, he was now running on the same White City track. This not only indicated his progress but also the significance of the inter-varsity sports at the time – the fact that the two institutions used such an august arena. Even so, according to Bannister, the track had 'the consistency of lumpy porridge' and the weather was cold. Yet he smashed (not simply broke) his personal best time, running 4m. 30.8s. This was an astonishing improvement and may have resulted from his more controlled running style. What's more, the 17-year-old freshman had won the inter-varsity race by 20 yards with a lung-bursting final sprint, having moved from third place to first round the last bend. It was considered the most noteworthy event of the afternoon and the BBC radio service thought it was worth mentioning on the six o'clock news. That evening, at the customary post-meeting party, he met Jack Lovelock, regarded by many as the consummate miler; but even Lovelock, the Olympic champion, could not replace Wooderson as Bannister's hero.

Victory in the Oxford–Cambridge clash had led the editor of the monthly magazine, *Athletics*, to suggest that the youthful Roger Bannister was a prospect for the 1948 Olympics. But of more immediacy was the fact that having won meant that he was considered a suitable representative of his university for its annual match with the AAA that took place at Iffley Road in early June. He was now 18 and growing in strength, speed and confidence. In this race he further lowered his best time to 4m. 24.6s, winning by ten yards. Now he was getting somewhere. For a youngster this was an impressive time, faster than his hero at the same age. He was on his way and soon represented the university abroad, one of the perks of being an Oxford man. He had a trip to the USA to compete for Oxford and Cambridge against Ivy League college athletes on the east coast. Oxford provided other things. He could consult the college coach, but insisted that he would work things out for himself. But perhaps above all, college life provided him with a growing confidence and, what's more, a goodly supply of cultural capital. Networks grew easily; they did not have to be made.

In late 1947, after what seemed to have been an incredibly short period of time since he had started running seriously, Bannister did indeed receive an invitation to become one of 15 'possibles' to represent Britain in the Olympic Games 1,500 metres race, to be held in London's Wembley Stadium in August of the following year. It would be the first Olympics since the Nazi Games of 1936 and London had stepped into the very large breach in which few capital cities felt capable of hosting such an event. On the basis of his best time, achieved in the Oxford v. AAA match, he was way down the European rankings' list, let alone the world's. In Sweden alone there were about 50 athletes who could have run faster. The AAA would provide the 'possibles' with certain kinds of assistance such as special coaching and food parcels – payment in kind – but they were hardly state athletes.

There are two versions of Bannister's attitude towards the 1948 Olympics. The *History of OUAC* suggests that he had gone all-out to win a place on the Games team. Bannister's own view was that he faced a dilemma. He was flattered to be listed as a 'possible' but at the time he was also wary, if not scared. After all, he was still only 18 years old. Was he emotionally immature? He might even have read the words of the Abrahams brothers that athletic precocity 'rarely results in ultimate athletic distinction: the price has to be paid for premature ripeness'. This was hardly a universal law but Bannister decided not to risk anything and declined the invitation, feeling that he should set the 1952 Games as his target. Even so, 1948 was to be a year of steady improvement, in terms of times. He took part in his second inter-varsity match, winning in 4m. 23.4s. He was becoming noticed and Jack Crump, one of the most powerful men in British athletics and team manager of the British Amateur Athletic Board (BAAB), said that every time he saw Bannister run, he became more and more impressed. He ran only slightly slower when just winning the universities' championships, an event in which he was almost overtaken by an Irish rugby player-cum-miler. This was a salutary reminder that he was far from invincible, even in university competitions.

In the early summer he ran in what was arguably his most difficult race so far. He was entered by the Achilles Club for the mile in the Kinnaird Trophy track meeting at Chiswick. This meeting included athletes from the major clubs in the Greater London area, bringing Bannister out of university competition and into the less cloistered world of inter-club athletics. He records that 'most of the race was a battle of elbows' and he was not quite ready for it; he was rather out of place. He allowed himself to get detached from the leading runners and finished fourth – but in a personal best time, estimated to be 4m. 18.7s.

Had he done the right thing by withdrawing from the Olympic selection? Now he was not so sure; after all by 1952 anything could happen. He wavered. His mind might be made up for him in his next race, the AAA championships at the White City Stadium. This propelled Bannister to higher levels than ever. It was possible that the race could be won in 4m. 10s – 50 yards ahead of what he could deliver. Two significant contenders were in the field. One was Bill Nankeville, an established British international and, after Wooderson, the fastest British miler ever; the other was Joseph Barthel, a runner from Luxemburg who was to surprise the athletics world four years later. Throughout the race Bannister hesitated pushing himself too hard, aware that several of the runners were much faster than him. Nankeville won in 4m. 14.2s, Bannister finishing fifth in yet another personal best time of 4m. 17.2s. He was the third British runner to finish, but Doug Wilson, the experienced international, did not run and was given the third Olympic place. Like the Kinnaird mile, this race had pitted Bannister against runners a notch or two above his standard. Now he realised what would be required and commented that he was 'relieved on the whole that I did not earn selection for the 1948 Olympics'. Even so, on the basis of his best time he was among the top 20 milers in Europe though it must be said that the mile was run less frequently than the 1,500 metres. If equivalent 1,500 metres times were included he would have been about the fiftieth fastest miler in the world at a time when standards were relatively low.

It is not immediately clear when Bannister first got a thirst for becoming the first man to run a mile in less than four minutes. But what sort of person could have such an ambition? Certainly not the casual runner or 'amateur'. Having watched the Olympic Games at Wembley in 1948 as assistant to the Commandant of the British team, Col. Evan A. Hunter, O.B.E. (a vacation job he easily slipped into, either through his athletic ability or his Oxford contacts – or both), he became fully aware that the milers from other parts of Europe were far superior to those in the UK. Despite the abrupt conclusion of the careers of Hägg and Andersson, the Swedes still tended to dominate the middle-distance running scene. At the 1948 Olympics they got three runners in the first five in the 1,500 metres final. In heavy rain and on a sodden track, Henry Eriksson won in 3m. 49.8s, followed closely by the well-known Lennart Strand, and Gunnar Bergkvist in fifth place (Figure 3.3). By 1950 seven of the top eight fastest milers of all time were Swedish

Figure 3.3 Henry Eriksson (right) defeats Lennart Strand in pouring rain at the 1948 Olympics 1,500 metres final, Wembley Stadium, London (author's collection)

– the lone non-Swede being Wooderson. Given the strength and power of the Nordic runners Bannister accepted that 'new targets had to be set and more vigorous training programmes prepared'. Aware that the next Olympics, in Helsinki, were four years away, he acknowledged that the two years before the Games would be dedicated to 'single-minded preparation' for the Olympic title. 'Targets', 'training programmes' and single-mindedness: connotations of seriousness, dedication, obsession, diligence, science.

A postscript for 1948 is, I think, worth recording. A somewhat odd feature of Oxbridge athletics is the continuation of track running into the winter months. I have already alluded to the Freshmen's meeting but additionally there is a relays meeting that has traditionally been held in what, for many, would be the middle of the cross-country season. In November 1948, at the inter-varsity relays match at Iffley Road, Bannister ran the final mile of the 4 × one mile relay in the same sort of time he had been running in the summer – 4m. 17.4s. This showed a remarkable ability to maintain his fitness. Jack Crump was there to record it and, with the London Olympics now out of the way, he stated that 'visions of Helsinki keep coming to my mind'. A mental map of Bannister's athletic future was being plotted.

Roger Bannister's assiduousness brought rewards. He continued to run cross-country and in the inter-varsity race finished joint second with J.F. Pollard, the winner being James Scott-Wilson. In fourth place was a Cambridge undergraduate named C.W. Brasher. In the annual Oxford–Cambridge track duel in March 1949, at the White City Stadium as usual, Bannister brought his best mile time down to 4m. 16.2s, at a time of the year before the European season had really started. In this race he not only led from the start but also demonstrated what was to become his trademark: his finishing burst that left his opponents floundering in his wake. His time also broke the inter-varsity record, set by the redoubtable C.C. Henderson-Hamilton as long ago as 1905.

Seeking to achieve a high level of fitness so early in the year was a tradition of Oxbridge athletics, given the brevity of the ancient universities' terms. His early season result attracted continental interest. The London correspondent of the Swedish sports newspaper, *Idrottsbladet*, witnessed his run at the White City track and reported that 'several experts rated him as the first four-minute miler' and while, to date, he had 'only' run 4m. 16.2s he looked impressive, 'though not the kind of runner who can go out alone after a record'. This turned out to be as accurate a prediction as one could expect. Later in 1949 Bannister lowered his half-mile time to 1m. 52.7s, a sign that his speed was to be reckoned with over two laps as well as four.

Given the seriousness and planning of Bannister's progress, it seems surprising that the 1950s have been seen by some as a golden age of recreational sport, pure in its amateurism and lack of seriousness. Experiments in the inhaling of oxygen before a race had taken place as early as 1908 and while in Britain the science of running was a world away from today's, numerous experiments were being carried out in Finland, the Soviet Union and Germany into applied sports science. And in the 1950s British athletes certainly knew about performance-enhancing substances, widespread in other sports – notably cycling – at that time. The British runner, Gordon Pirie claimed that athletes of *many* nations were probably addicted to stimulants, though concrete evidence was hard to find. But there was, he added, plenty of circumstantial evidence. He recalls that a doctor asked him what stimulants he used. He denied that he took them, upon which the medico replied 'Well, you must be one of the few mugs who don't'. Pirie claims to have *frequently* observed runners sniffing inhalants, 'presumably benzedrine', and at one international meeting a well-known doctor came into the dressing room before a race and asked the British competitors if any of them wanted 'any little pills' (i.e. 'pep pills'). Indeed, in the 1950s, inhaled amphetamine was readily available in Britain without prescription. And Pirie was pretty adamant that 'sudden staggering performances quite out of keeping with known form can only be explained by the use of drugs'.

The concern with enhancing performance was, I suggest, nothing more than the way athletics was moving, with Nurmi as its most obvious point of departure. Indeed, the taking of stimulants seems to be a logical part of the extreme achievement orientation to which top-class runners could (and can) become addicted. And the scientific tenor of the times was reflected in the growing number of predictions that were made about ultimate performances. In 1951 the oddball Australian coach, Percy Cerutty, wrote that 3m. 53s should be considered a normal attainment for running the mile. In other words, with the right training, such a time should pose no problems. A more restrained estimate appeared in the sober pages of the BBC's *The Listener* which (with hindsight) conservatively predicted that the world record for the mile might be as low as 3m. 58s by the year 2000. It arrived much earlier than that.

Among the benefits of being an Oxford sportsman was that travelling to foreign countries was almost regarded as the norm. As a freshman Roger Bannister had been a member of an Oxford team that toured Germany. He visited the USA in 1949 with a combined Oxford and Cambridge team who took on the elite US universities of Cornell and Princeton. At Princeton he met the melancholy Jack Lovelock who was then working in New York but was to die on the electric rails of the New York subway just before the end of the year. Lovelock's depression, in his fortieth year, was counterpoised by Bannister's vitality. At Princeton he further lowered his best mile time to 4m. 11.1s, the fastest time ever achieved by a 20-year-old. He was now on the verge of world class, and by the end of the year he was the second fastest miler in Britain after Bill Nankeville and thirteenth fastest in the world that year – phenomenal progress in view of the fact that it was less than four years ago that he ran his first ever mile. The next obvious target was 4m. 10s. He had maintained his winter engagement with cross-country and climaxed his harrier career when winning the inter-varsity cross-country race, narrowly beating his Cambridge adversary, D.H. Gilbert, by three seconds.

The modern sports-worker is always on the move and in 1950 Bannister became a global athlete, traversing the world like a modern jet-setter, a sporting globetrotter. He would certainly have been selected for the Empire Games, being held in February in New Zealand but was prevented from doing so by the priority of university examinations. It was his fourth and final year at Exeter College. But once academic requirements were over he was off on the grand tour. First stop was Finland, following an invitation from Helsinki University, and useful in view of the fact that the 1952 Olympics were being held in that fine city. While there he ran 1,500 metres at Kouvala in 3m. 57s – roughly equivalent to the mile times he had been running in England. In the same year, as a member of an Achilles Club team, he ran in Greece, seeing the ancient home of athletics and the 1896 Olympic stadium where the modern Olympics were first held. But the big event of the year was the European championships, held in Brussels. Bannister had been concentrating on the half-mile and had been selected for the 800 metres – his first big international event. His rise from novice to championship athlete, in an event that he did not regard as his speciality, was remarkable. His best half-mile time was by now 1m. 52.1s, achieved in coming second in the AAA championships behind the great Jamaican runner, Arthur Wint, who had won a silver medal in the 800 metres at the London Olympics, a feat he was to repeat in Helsinki. Bannister's time was very good by British standards though three seconds (over 20 yards) slower than Wooderson's national record.

The European 800 metres championship exposed Bannister to the jostling and scrambling of the international championship race. The final started with an astonishingly fast first lap by the Norwegian, Auden Boysen, who covered the first circuit in 50.9s, faster than Bannister's personal best for the distance (Figure 3.4). But Bannister, in his first major race held his place in the pack, hanging back in the early stages. As the race progressed his speed brought him up to the shoulders of the leading runners, the other British finalist, John Parlett, a half-mile specialist, and the Frenchman, Marcel Hansenne. Bannister's swift but

Figure 3.4 Soon after the start of the 800 metres final, European Championships, 1950, Brussels. Auden Boysen of Norway is in the lead, Bannister is number 305 (*Athletics Weekly*, photograph by kind permission of Descartes Publishing Limited)

ungainly final strides brought him to the tape, shoulder to shoulder with Hansenne. It appeared to be a dead heat for second place but the judges, having consulted the photo finish, deemed Bannister had got third place. Both runners were given a time of 1m. 50.7s. For Bannister, this was the equivalent of knocking half a second off his best 880 yards time. Shrewd observers of the sport spotted Bannister's 800 metres speed and noted that, on the basis of times, he was faster than any of the world's best milers – Hägg, Andersson and Strand.

The 'scrambling' that Bannister experienced at Brussels was a form of competition that involved physical contact in the form of elbowing and random spiking. It appeared to be anathema to Bannister – too messy and untidy and rather too much like handicap racing where there were always runners getting in the way. In overtaking such runners, he would run further than he needed, adding to the time taken to complete an event. As a result, he felt that one of the problems of handicap racing was that 'accurate timing' was difficult in such races. He also disliked large fields of athletes in track races, believing that the maximum should be eight in any race over 1,500 metres or a mile: 'This would give the competitors the best possible chance of running instead of scrambling ... and for those [like himself] who are stop-watch minded the time would be faster'. The central concerns were time, the stop-watch, and limited numbers of opponents, typical of modern thinking. Time mattered; slowness was anathema. Bannister seemed to have wanted some kind of pure space, uncontaminated by opponents who might get in his way. The anaesthetised laboratory of the paced experiment was clearly the ideal.

After Brussels, Bannister took part in a meeting in Paris where Parlett again beat him over 800 metres. After this event he decided that it was time to distance himself from the city and the machine (and the stadium, the racing and the modern) and explore France as a hitchhiker. His yearning for the countryside never left him and he returned to England refreshed – for more action on the (t)rack. What is of some social significance, however, was that Bannister was able to indulge in such wanderings without any serious concern about a salary or a job. On a previous occasion he had 'decided' that he needed a holiday in Ireland – and simply took it.

The climax of 1950 was an end-of-year trip to New Zealand with a small British team to take part in the Centennial Games. In New Zealand and Australia, grass tracks were the norm. Frequently on cricket pitches, they were often immaculately manicured and, at their best, probably as fast as good cinder tracks. In Christchurch where the meeting was held, Bannister faced the Australian miler Don Macmillan who, later, was to assist him in different circumstances. It was raining heavily on the day of the race and the meeting was postponed. A day later, with the grass track still very wet, Bannister won in a personal best time, 4m. 9.9s – he had got under 4m. 10s. What could he achieve on a well-prepared cinder track? He was now the third fastest British miler ever, after his hero Wooderson and his rival Nankeville. He was now on the brink of world class. Taking the year's 1,500 metres times into account he would have ranked about the twenty-fifth fastest miler in the world.

Roger Bannister, now on a postgraduate course at Merton College, had learned three things from the Brussels championship and other international encounters. The first was that he had run several races where he had clocked good times but had not won. This was not good enough; he needed greater strength and that would come from consistent training, reflecting a more 'professional' approach. Second, exposure to international events caused more strain, nervousness and tension than the university events on which he had been brought up. There was also the over-explicit nationalism in the uniforms and flags. He was running for his nation and this did not always square with his personal ambitions. It was a widespread feeling at the time that nationalism was ruining sport and that state support smacked of communism. A third thing he learned was that constant travelling as a star athlete had its downside and was not as glamorous as those at home might have thought. In two months in 1950 he had competed in six European countries but saw little of any of them. After all, one 400 metres circuit is much like any other. He commented in frustration, 'I might just as well have run all my races at the White City in London'. He would have to condition himself to the mechanical nature of globalised running, the standardised track as an analogue of the assembly line from which records were produced.

PLANNING, TRAINING AND THE OLYMPICS

Planning is not a word that slips lightly from the lips of a 'gentleman amateur' but planning is exactly what Bannister did in the years, months, days, hours and minutes leading up to the four-minute mile. The place, the race and the pace were all planned in advance. As early as 1948 Bannister stated that the Iffley Road track at Oxford would be the site for his greatest races. At that time he was president – the youngest ever – of the OUAC. The old Iffley Road track, with its large laps and marked slope was clearly outmoded. How Jack Lovelock had run 4m. 12s on such a track was beyond the comprehension of those runners who had to finish a race uphill. Bannister was determined to get the track updated, with six lanes and a level surface of 440 yards (Figure 3.5). Old 'Blues' complained about this plan and penned letters to *The Times* about it but Bannister prevailed and having done so stated that he would choose it for his biggest races, seemingly unaware that the locations of some of these races would be beyond his control.

During the early 1950s Bannister devoured new training ideas and experiences from a range of sources. In his early days at Oxford his training consisted of a lot of track running with cross-country thrown in during the winter. Track running can become boring and he became aware of the *fartlek* method, beloved by Hägg and Andersson. He

Figure 3.5 Iffley Road: the new track under construction, 1948

modified his training methods along these lines, not aping them uncritically, but accepting the elements of *fartlek* that would suit him best. As I have shown, he improved his tactical and speed skills during 1950 by concentrating on half-mile racing, not winning many races but gaining experience and demonstrating his prowess at a major championship event. He saw this as a scientist and termed it an 'experiment'. Indeed, every race, for Bannister, was an experiment. He learned that he needed more strength, which, he said 'could only come from consistent training'. Again, the scientist and the athlete became one. He realised that the 'objectivity and care' of the laboratory carried over into his running. As he commented, 'I began to prepare my training programme and to test my physical reactions with the same precision that I had learnt in the laboratory'. In his contribution to a book on training methods he stated that the 'peak performance, whether this be at the school sports or a national championship, can only be achieved as a result of *hard training* and careful *planning*' (italics added). The 'gentleman amateur'? Hardly.

Working in a laboratory enabled Bannister to mix his academic research with his personal training regimen. In the lab. he used a motor-driven treadmill on which the speed and gradient could be changed in order to exhaust the athlete in a few minutes. He said, 'In time I learnt to repeat my performance on the treadmill so that I could study the effect on my performances of changes in body temperature, in the acidity of the blood, and in the composition of the air breathed in'. He experimented on himself, inhaling air enriched with oxygen at either 66 per cent or 100 per cent. He found exercise substantially easier when the percentage was 66 per cent. Breathing seemed effortless and he stopped as a result of boredom rather than exhaustion. Bannister's supervisor D.J.C. Cunningham, and his friend Norris McWhirter, also took part, with similar results. In summary, Bannister observed that 'while breathing the ambient fresh air, signs of fatigue make their appearance about the seventh or eighth minute afterwards as against 22 or 23 minutes after taking the oxygen'. McWhirter claimed that he could have run indefinitely had he not had to catch a train! Additionally, he said that for Bannister the four-minute mile was like a day off compared with training on this remorseless machine: hardly the 'common sense' training of a 'gentleman amateur'.

Bannister's use of *fartlek* was supplemented by the more track-based method known as interval running, a method which he felt built up speed and stamina simultaneously. This style of running had been made famous by the German coach, Waldemar Gerschler, who had coached the German 400 and 800 metres superstar, Rudolf Harbig, who was killed on the Eastern Front as a member of the German army (and the Nazi Party). On a trip to Germany Bannister and his friends had briefly met Gerschler, who was Director of Physical Education at Freiburg University, and were impressed with his approach. Many observers still regard interval running as the most mechanistic of training methods. In his book, *Sport and Work*, the German sociologist, Bero Rigauer, described it as 'a periodic alternation between exertion and recovery or between work and pause'. Neo-marxists love it because they see it as creating an alienated human body being subjected to a machine-like regime, its aim being increased efficiency. The body is trained in the production of results. It made sport seem like work, the athlete being the object of time and motion study by his trainer or, in Bannister's case, self-administering the disciplined body – submitting himself to new regimens of training. Interval running, he wrote, 'is the basis of modern training'.

Training may produce fitness but for the athlete a race is needed to see if it has produced a result. In 1951 Bannister had been training hard and needed a race to test himself. Fortunately, he was invited to the USA to compete in the so-called 'Benjamin Franklin Mile' at the Penn Relays in Philadelphia. He tested his ability by inviting himself to a low-key inter-club meeting at Motspur Park between Imperial College and Walton Athletic Club, of which Chataway was a member. A three-quarters of a mile race had been arranged and he sensed he could break the British record. It was the first of numerous occasions that

Chris Chataway agreed to pace him, on this occasion until the last lap. Bannister ran the three laps progressively faster, ending up with a time of 2m. 56.8s, finishing not unduly distressed. This was only one-fifth of a second short of Andersson's world record and nearly three seconds faster than Wooderson's British best. The 50 or so spectators had got an unexpected treat. The British press was highly impressed. The four-minute mile was on the cards. If he hadn't realised it before with the sub-4m. 10s mile, he now knew for sure that he was a world-class athlete.

Bannister's trip to Pennsylvania was eventful. It was not simply that he further lowered his personal best to 4m. 8.3s; he also became embroiled in a situation that was to be held against him by other British runners. The BAAB usually insisted on athletes being accompanied when they travelled overseas. This was old fashioned paternalism but was justified because of the supposed possibility of complications that may arise when an Englishman is abroad. Bannister got special permission to go to America on the grounds that it was not solely an athletic visit. He would also visit laboratories at the University of Pennsylvania in connection with his scientific studies. He was also experienced in travelling overseas, given the international nature of the Oxford athletic calendar. A possible slip of the pen led him to observe that he 'went over with two jobs to do instead of one'. His allusion to running as a 'job' was, I presume, metaphorical. Or was this a suggestion of Bannister's 'professional' approach? Some other British runners felt that this business of being able to travel abroad without supervision was a privilege that they were denied. It served to sustain the difference between the 'ordinary' athlete and the Oxbridge crowd: as if they didn't have enough advantages already.

Following the new personal best, Bannister had great success with his running throughout the pre-Olympic season, reverting to the mile for almost all his races. Sub-4m. 10s was now normal and he reduced his best time to 4m. 7.8s when winning the annual AAA championship. He was becoming much more than a national figure. His global visibility was reflected in him being rated the number one miler of the year in the American *Track and Field News* annual world rankings.

I have tried to show that Bannister trained hard, used scientific principles, and treated each race as an experiment. But it was the image of a 'gentleman amateur' that got projected to the great British public and to academic writers on sport. One such scholar has described Bannister as having 'the amateur, almost offhand, approach to training' and such a perceived lightness of training led some observers to aver that he was a poor role model for younger athletes. The question of his training had come to a head in late 1951 when he went semi-public in completing a 'questionnaire', a regular feature in *Athletics Weekly*. His response to one of the first questions – what was his objective in athletics? – was that he wanted to 'get the most out of myself': a brief reply but one that contained nothing but achievement orientation. He went on to claim that he trained for three-quarters of an hour, three days a week (though in his book, *First Four Minutes*, he stated that in the early 1950s it was four days). His responses to the various questions were brief in the extreme, curt to the point of being uninformative. Some seemed flippant. In response to a question about the part played by coaching, he commented: 'Have received help from many friends'. His admissions about the content of his training were equally brief and opaque. He alluded to his regular test, a time trial at ten-day intervals in the period leading up to a mile race. When no serious races were on the horizon he ran five miles at various speeds on grass (i.e. *fartlek*). He also pointed out that training, when the athlete doesn't feel like running, is often valueless and may be harmful.

Bannister's thoughts on his training were met with a blitz of letters to the editor and were the subject of correspondence for two or three weeks. The first respondent, one Hazel Needham, felt that his responses were 'brief almost to the point of being *non est*' and served no useful purpose. She wanted 'concrete details of the athlete's ideas and methods of training'. The editor responded, saying that he had returned the questionnaire to Bannister 'with a request for more information but the published details were all that he was prepared to give'. Now Bannister felt duty-bound to reply, saying that there was a reason for his brevity. He wrote, 'I feel that there is a real danger of athletes tending to follow too closely a rigid training schedule'. Individualism was all-important. The athlete should love running, not be forced into a regimen that may not suit him. Basically, what he actually did in training depended on how he felt and he never decided what he was going to do until he had warmed up and tested his 'freshness and inclination'. Some letters suggested that Bannister was too light-hearted and relaxed about his training – 'a very haphazard affair'; other respondents strongly supported his approach, noting that he had done pretty well on it so far, implicitly justifying an 'amateur' approach based on character and pluck. But one prophet of doom observed that, while Bannister was potentially the best miler in the world, he had 'yet to be convinced that he knows enough about conditioning himself to beat the world's best at Helsinki'. And there the correspondence ended.

The suggestion of light training in the Corinthian mode, was, to a large extent, the legacy of the Oxford tradition of not being seen to push oneself too hard, neither in scholarship nor in sports. Industrious scholars – 'trogs' or 'grey men' – were frequently disliked, even despised. Bannister's response to the questionnaire may well have been flippant with a residual undergraduate licence to be economical with the truth. He later wrote:

> Undergraduates are, without exception, haunted by the fear of being thought to take anything too seriously. I know that I developed the pose of apparent indifference, to hide the tremendous enthusiasm which I felt for running from the day I set foot in Oxford. You had to be careful in Oxford not to appear to take games too seriously as you had at school to avoid the stigma of being called a 'swot'.

The contrived image, or the invented tradition, of the leisured amateur was confirmed by his university friend Chris Chataway who made it clear that 'Roger went to *great lengths* to conceal the amount of training he did ... he did more than he said he did' (italics added). And Bannister reciprocated with regards to Chataway who, he said, 'always gave an impression that running seemed to come a poor second to life in general. This air of casualness overlaid his *intense* interest in running and the *very serious* training he actually performed' (italics added).

For Bannister, the 1952 Olympics were the major target of his career so far. Despite the accusations of haphazardness, he had, in his own words, developed an 'Olympic plan'. Running was teaching him the need to make decisions, to have a positive attitude. Most of his winter training was done on grass. He often ran round the smooth cricket field of the posh Harrow School, near his home. Often this was under cover of darkness and he felt his lone body seemingly move faster in the dark. The sensuousness of the experience exhilarated him. In spring and summer he would do more track training where he could hone his speed. He raced sparingly and before each mile race prepared himself with a three-quarters of a mile time trial. By modern standards his training *was* light, though not nearly as light as was sometimes thought. But the 'plan' did not exclude short periods when Bannister felt he had to get back to nature. He was a hobbyist rock climber and with Chris Brasher would sometimes go off to Snowdonia in 'wild' Wales for a break from the routine of the training schedule and the quarter-mile track. This can be seen, I suppose, as being at odds with the extreme regimen of training undertaken by one of his contemporaries, Gordon Pirie, the up and coming middle-distance runner who modelled his training on his hero, the Czech, Emil Zátopek (the 'human locomotive'). It is said that when Pirie ran badly he trained harder. When Bannister got fed up with running he rested. He did not want to take disciplined enjoyment too far. But resting in the mountain air was really all part of the plan. It was like a school playtime, a factory tea break, a summer vacation: enough of a break to prepare the body for more work. Like many runners, Bannister saw his body as a machine and felt that it should be treated as such.

Throughout the Olympic season Bannister experienced a love–hate relationship with the British press. The editor of *Athletics Weekly*, P.W. 'Jimmy' Green, rated Bannister 'the greatest potential miler in the world' but again criticised his 'lone wolf' approach to training. He was also noted as a relative novice and Green favoured a young German, Werner Lueg, for the gold medal. Bannister was seen as keeping to his own (inappropriate) training plans and was not willing to divulge them. As a future world record holder for the mile, Derek Ibbotson, later put it, he 'sometimes appeared the Greta Garbo of the track'. He didn't want to run in the AAA mile championship, keeping everything he had in check, like a spring waiting to uncoil in the Helsinki final. He was accused of avoiding his rivals, limiting his public appearances, and not willing to have himself coached. He would plough a lonely furrow – the individualist, striving to 'get the last ounce out' of himself in Finland. He would show them; he sought status through achievement. He ran a few races over the half-mile and showed good form in winning the AAA championship at this event. Shortly after he ran another half-mile and was beaten in a slow race by Albert Webster, generally regarded as a journeyman athlete compared with Bannister. The press response was that they had been proved right; his lack of racing experience had let him down. Some fans enjoyed the sense of *Schadenfreude* induced by his defeat while some cynics said that he lost it deliberately to escape the publicity. Bannister's selection for the Olympic team, without going through the unofficial trial of the AAA championships, again made him unpopular with other athletes and fans. They felt that the Oxford background favoured him, that he was the selector's pet. 'Gentleman amateur' or not, he did not lack controversy.

At about the same time, the young German, Lueg, equalled Hägg's and Strand's world record for 1,500 metres of 3m. 43s and was again tipped to become the first four-minute miler. But the closer the Games got, the more Bannister was touted as favourite for the Olympic title, by at least some of the experts. Norris and Ross McWhirter (who, in

1951, had together authored an excellent statistical history of world athletics entitled *Get to Your Marks!*) had established a monthly magazine, *Athletics World*, for athletics fanatics and collectors of statistics. They got five famous pundits to predict who would get medals in the Helsinki 1,500 metres race. Three predicted Bannister as the gold medallist; only one felt that he wouldn't get any kind of medal. Yet he had not run faster than 4m. 10s during the 1952 season. He 'has so much confidence he doesn't bother to test himself against top flight competition', raved *Track and Field News*, also positioning him as the favourite.

The elevation of Bannister to preferred candidate for the Olympic gold medal at the age of 23, was, for those who knew about it, strongly supported by a fantastic time trial he undertook at Motspur Park, ten days before the Olympic final. As previously, his ploy was to time himself over three-quarters of a mile. On this occasion, as he had done previously and would do on several subsequent occasions, he asked his friend and future world 5,000 metres record holder, Chris Chataway to pace him for about 660 yards. Bannister was full of running, each lap faster than the previous one. He ended up finishing with a time of 2m. 52.9s – as far as was known, the fastest ever recorded and, arguably, the best result he would ever achieve. He rated the three-quarter mile his best distance but it was rarely run as a competitive event. But the Olympic 1,500 would only be 320 yards longer. He now felt confident of winning a gold medal and breaking the world record at the same time. He bound those who had witnessed the time trial to keep it secret, not wanting to add to the pressure of public expectations fuelled by a British press greedy for Olympic gold.

The days before the Olympics were eventful, and in the short term disastrous and confidence-sapping. The original arrangement of the 1,500 metres was that there would be heats, a day's rest and then the final. This, Bannister felt, was reasonable; he reckoned he could handle it. However, within little more than a week before the event was to take place he opened his morning paper to discover that there were to be semi-finals for his chosen event. This meant three races in three days!

He was shattered. This was not part of the game plan. A fine-tuned athlete like him was dependent on 24 hours recovery between two vital races. He was sure that all his main opponents had been training more regularly and with greater intensity than him; in other words, he had the excuses ready before the race had even started. He travelled to Helsinki with Chataway, five days before the heats.

The stadium, holding 60,000 spectators, was built originally with the aborted 1940 Olympics in mind. It is a splendid, typically Nordic structure built of white stone with an impressive tower, in the style of Alvar Aalto. As in Turku, a statue of Nurmi is found on the approach to the entrance, just to remind visitors of Finnish running traditions (see Figure 2.1). The 1952 Olympics were presented to the public as a Cold War battle, between the US and the USSR. Finland was an appropriate location, balanced precariously between East and West. Bannister faced his own personal battles – to perform well and rid himself of the double psychological stress of coping with the extra race and satisfying the British dream of an Olympic gold medal.

The first heat was easy enough; Bannister qualified for the next round in third place in a slow time, though he was required to sprint a fast last lap. The second round was tighter; he crossed the line in fifth place, in line with three other athletes and again needing a fast final lap to make it. Most of those expected to do so had made it to the final. The German, Lueg, the co-holder of the world's record was there; so too were the (allegedly) chain-smoking Finn, Denis Johansson, the fast Norwegian, Auden Boysen, the Algerian, running for France, Mohamed (Patrick) El Mabrouk and Bob McMillen of the USA. Sweden was represented by Åberg and Eriksson. Other, less well-known runners, made up the complement of 12 who would toe the line. Among those who looked promising in the heats was Joseph Barthel from Luxemburg, studying at Harvard but trained by Gerschler from Germany. A conspicuous absentee was Gaston Reiff. The Belgian had favoured his chances in the 5,000 metres but having qualified for the final dropped out after 4,000 metres.

Bannister slept poorly in the days leading up to the final. A sympathiser with his plight was The Right Honourable Philip Noel-Baker, a former cabinet minister and silver medallist in the 1920 Antwerp Olympics, who was the nation's major advocate of the writings of Pierre de Coubertin, founder of the modern Olympics. As President of the Achilles Club, members were able to benefit freely from Noel-Baker's advice, influence and in some cases patronage. He often corresponded with Bannister about tactics and such like. Noel-Baker was something of an insomniac and took sleeping pills. He considered offering them to Bannister but didn't – not because of the possible infringement of drug or doping conventions, but because they might have a negative effect. Bannister was nervous as well as tired. There was a sense of tension in the dressing room as the finalists assembled for their third race in three days. Out in the arena, the knowledgeable Finnish crowd awaited the race that their hero, Nurmi, had so dominated.

The start was announced and the runners went to their marks. Then Eriksson, tense and anxious, false started, further unsettling the other runners. At the second time of asking they were off, and the German, Lamers led for the first lap, Bannister in fourth or fifth place. The 800 metres point was reached in 2m. 2.1s and at 900 metres Lueg strode to the front and opened a two-yard gap. The bell sounded for the last lap and a mad rush took Barthel, El Mabrouk, Lamers, Bannister and McMillen striding along the back straight. As the runners rounded the bend coming into the final straight, Lueg was still in the lead, seemingly unassailable. The slight, balding figure of Barthel followed with McMillen, Bannister and El Mabrouk almost shoulder to shoulder, the Algerian having to run wide in the second lane. Lueg was feeling the effect of his early effort and the others inexorably closed on him. It was Barthel who just squeezed out McMillen for the Olympic title with Lueg third. Bannister was just behind in the dreaded fourth place, utterly exhausted, disappointed, distraught, devastated. The last-minute change in the racing conditions were to blame but he put a brave face on it, recalling the Olympic slogan about the important thing being to take part. Alongside this gesture, however, he observed that the gold medal had gone to the strongest rather than the fastest. To this, the editor of *Athletics Weekly*, sharp as ever, retorted that track racing is a sport for the tough as much as for the speedy. On the same subject, Bannister was later to write, in *The Listener*, how sport 'shakes our roots with its confusing pattern of success and failure. What a very thin line divides the two'.

In their report of the race in *Athletics World*, the McWhirters still rated Lueg as the prime contender for the four-minute mile rather than the first and second placers who had each recorded the same time of 3m. 45.2s, an Olympic record. Bannister, they observed, had looked listless, unable to reproduce anything like the form he had displayed to his intimates a week or so before at Motspur Park. Noel-Baker felt that if he had slept well before the race he would have won. The Olympics, with heats, semi-finals and final were, as Bannister had learned, a different world from one-off time trials.

The 1952 Olympics were a massive learning experience for Roger Bannister. The power of press hype was brought home to him in a brutal way, as was the recognition that he represented Great Britain through his track results. His individualism was straight-jacketed. He was a kind of national representation whose performances were thought to reflect the condition of the nation, whose flag he wore on his running vest and blazer. He also realised that his strength was lacking, in comparison with some of his opponents who seemed better prepared to handle the heavy racing schedule of a major championship.

He received more criticism from the British press – a failure who had let the nation down. Indeed, the British athletics team *per se* was regarded as a disaster. Alan Hoby of the *Sunday Express* thought that we 'should lower the flag to fly at half-mast'; Maurice Smith of *The People* blurted out that 'right now I feel like suing British athletes for breach of contract'. And from the USA the editor of *Track and Field News* felt that Bannister lacked the competitive temperament. Yet he had got fourth place in an Olympic final at the age of 23. What's more, his time of 3m. 46s was a British record and, if roughly converted into an equivalent mile time it was 4m. 4s. He had broken Lovelock's Olympic record. What if it *had* been over a mile as a straight race, without the preliminaries? Given that three-quarter mile time he had surely been in four-minute mile form in 1952.

The Olympics used metric measurements and during July and much of August the world of athletics ignored the imperial measures. But more than a hint that the four-minute mile was looking vulnerable – or at least approachable – was flagged in Antwerp a few weeks after the Games. The Belgian runner, Gaston Reiff, getting his act together after having failed to finish in the Olympic 5,000 metres, recorded a mile time of 4m. 2.8s. This made him the third fastest runner of all time, even though he was running slower than Andersson in 1943.

Despite the disappointment of Helsinki, Bannister did try to cash in on the undoubted fitness that he possessed before the Olympics. He asked an up-and-coming junior runner, Brian Hewson, to help him break Wooderson's national mile record. Hewson's task was to act as a pacemaker for the first two-and-a-half laps, a job he executed with little trouble. Once Bannister was on his own he appeared to fade and struggle. He just won the race but in a slow time of 4m. 13.8s, despite the fact that Hewson had run the first half-mile in 2m. 4s. Bannister was well past his annual peak and the record attempt was a post-Olympic anticlimax.

Things were rather different in Australia. John Landy, a 22-year-old student of agricultural science with a best mile time of 4m. 10s, had also competed in the Helsinki 1,500 metres but had been eliminated during the heats. By the end of 1952, in the Antipodean summer, he had somehow improved his ability substantially. He had taken advice from the maverick Aussie coach Percy Cerutty but soon lost faith in such an unpredictable character. In any case, his scientific background and the tips he had picked up while in Europe had encouraged a greater interest in interval running than in Cerutty's hippy-style beach, surf and sand dune approach. Changing his training methods, he soon found it easy to beat his best time in training. In a race in Melbourne, in windy conditions and on a poor track, Landy amazed the world of track and field by returning a mile time of 4m. 2.1s – over seven seconds faster than his previous best. It was run at a relatively even pace and was a stunning effort. Sceptics thought it either a fluke or that the track was short. However, a few weeks later, on 3 January 1953, he confirmed his presence as a serious contender for the four-minute mile with another fast time, 4m. 2.8s.

DAILY TRAINING AND BRITISH RECORDS

The Olympics came and went. Life went on. Despite his disappointment, Bannister's 1952 season was hardly a regression. Determined to make amends for his relative 'failure' at Helsinki he made a conscious shift to focus his attention less on winning races and more on achieving a time – that of under four minutes for the mile. Recognising the significance of even-paced running he became even more familiar with the use of pacemakers. As I have shown in my discussion of the Swedish athletes, the attempts on the mile record were often simply that – they were hardly races – with a predictable winner following an assigned pacemaker. The exception, of course, was when the two giants of the track, Hägg and Andersson clashed, but even here pacemakers were there to help them on their way. And it seems no accident that Bannister, a scientist, should employ the human analogue of the scientific pacemaker.

Several of Bannister's rivals received scientific training. Joseph Barthel, and his English contemporary Pirie, were trained by Waldemar Gerschler and Professor Herbert Reindel. But whereas these runners were trained by scientists, Bannister *was* a scientist and could, like Dr Jack Lovelock, use himself as a guinea pig. To have a coach was suitable for some but Bannister claimed to be his own man. He had a contretemps with the old Oxford coach, Bill Thomas, who had guided Lovelock but Bannister didn't like his 'do as I tell you' style.

The idea that Roger Bannister only trained three days a week *may* have been true during the late 1940s but by the time he had moved from Oxford to London in 1952 for an internship at St Mary's Hospital, he stated that he was training 'every day' at the black 440 yards cinder circuit at Paddington recreation ground, round the corner from Maida Vale tube station. It was a nondescript place, much like many of the other municipal parks scattered throughout greater London, with a public running track and changing rooms included. It was not only a change of location. He also became more sociable, training with a group. Training for racing now provided camaraderie − a group they called the 'Paddington lunch time club'. Bannister was very happy with the friendships he made there, impossible in the relative loneliness of his previous training. The anonymous Paddington track 'came to mean almost as much' to him as his beloved Iffley Road. His period in London included training that was hard and intensive. His Achilles Club colleague, Chris Brasher, made him work hard with his interval running. The daily training could, of course, become a daily grind and from time to time he and his acquaintances might take off for rock climbing in Scotland.

If British observers continued to describe him as akin to a dilettante athlete, he was represented differently in, at least, the *New York Times*. In an overview article on Bannister's training the *Times* reported that 'he altered the structure of his heart, and his muscles by *severe training*. All the time, he was keeping close scientific observation of himself in the *coldly detached* way of a medico'. Later, Arthur Daley wrote in the same paper that 'by *punishing* his body he toughened it and thereby increased its recovery rate' (my italics). Daley's compatriot, Ken Doherty, believed Bannister to have 'a rigorous training program'. And in the early months of 1953 a 'reliable source' had told the marathon runner, Jim Peters, that Bannister was having a seven-mile run every day. There's nothing in these observations to suggest an 'amateur', gentlemanly or otherwise. On the contrary, he was developing a culture of hardness, essential for success in the modern world of sport.

Sticking to his promise to have his important races at Iffley Road, Bannister embarked on a serious attempt to break, at least, some sort of mile record on 2 May 1953. He was a patriot and, he surely thought, what a wonderful contribution to Coronation Year it would be if he could break the four-minute barrier for Britain. The mile event was part of the annual meeting between Oxford University and a team assembled by the AAA. There was a clear plan: Chris Chataway, having replaced Bannister as president of OUAC, would lead for the first three laps, leaving Bannister to take over as soon as Chataway fell away, which he did, and dropped out, just before the beginning of the final 440 yards. Bannister surged ahead with no other runner remotely in contention. He strode to the finishing line, recording 4m. 3.6s, in so doing demolishing Wooderson's British record (Figure 3.6). Each of the four laps was faster than the previous one, Bannister showing impressive form in windy conditions. But the existence of the mythical target meant that Bannister still had to improve on his best time by one second per lap. Time was of the essence in more ways than one. Others might get there first. Time was running out and another record had to be broken.

British sports fans thought that an international mile at the so-called 'British Games' at the White City Stadium in late May might be the appropriate occasion. However, the race revealed the fickleness of the fans, on the one hand, and the inability of Bannister to run a fast time without a willing pacemaker, on the other. A section of the crowd booed and jeered as he sprinted to an easy victory in ideal conditions but in 4m. 9.4s, revealing that for at least a section of the British public, their admiration lay elsewhere. The jeers, apparently, came from devotees of the sport (that is, club runners and long-time enthusiasts) rather than from the broader, less-informed public who had come solely to see the new star, and hopefully a record in the process. Perhaps this crowd behaviour also reflected an anti-Oxbridge feeling. The race was a 'disappointing affair', moaned the *Athletics Weekly* reporter.

On 6 June at Compton, California, on a clear night at the California Relays, a Kansas University student, Wesley Santee (Figure 3.7) lined up for the mile. Santee, like Bannister had returned from Helsinki with

Figure 3.6 Roger Bannister breaks the British mile record, Iffley Road, Oxford, 1953 (author's collection)

nothing but experience. He was eliminated in the 5,000 metres heats in a slow time. Now things were different and *Track and Field News* reckoned that he would run 3m. 58s – someday. His coach, Bill Easton, predicted an even faster time. The field for the Compton mile was strong and Santee was rubbing shoulders with the likes of the aforementioned Reiff and the Finnish star, Denis Johansson. Santee ran with the pack until just before half way which was reached in 2m. 5.2s. Then he took off *à la* Cunningham and with a remarkably sustained sprint won in 4m. 2.3s.

Figure 3.7 Wesley Santee (Courtesy of the Athletic Department, University of Kansas)

Things were speeding up and Santee planned another attempt at the record in Dayton, Ohio in June. Bannister, knowing of the American's plan, agreed to take part in a craftily arranged pre-emptive strike by running a mile five hours before Santee. A hastily planned event – 'a special invitation mile' – was arranged during the lunch-break of the hardly auspicious Surrey Schools Championships, being held at Motspur Park on 27 June. This was surely one of the most incongruous athletic events ever staged in Britain. Only three runners took part. Apart from Bannister, there was an Australian Olympian Don Macmillan who was studying in London, and Bannister's friend, Chris Brasher, at the time the second best British steeplechase runner. They turned up in a mysterious black car. Schoolchildren mixed with dignitaries, notably Philip Noel-Baker, who had considered assisting Bannister at Helsinki.

After discussions with Noel-Baker in the changing rooms, the race was ready to start. Again, Bannister put the pacemaker mode of running into action. Macmillan set off at a world record pace and led for two and a half laps. Brasher, on the other hand, jogged round for two laps, hardly breathing until he loomed up ahead of Bannister, but a lap behind. In front but behind him, Brasher increased his pace and shouted words of encouragement, looking back over his shoulder, as he ran ahead, preventing himself from being lapped. Some of the schools' competitors, watching the three mature runners going through this charade, seem to have thought that Brasher had won and cheered wildly. But few of them could have known that Bannister had run the third fastest mile of all-time – 4m. 2s – the fastest in the world for eight years and run at almost even pace. With no pool of pressmen to interview him, Bannister cooled down and dashed off with a friend in a sporty vehicle for a weekend's hill-climbing in North Wales.

Fleet Street hacks read this result as a further indication of Bannister's secrecy about his training. *The Times*, told about the race by a 'friendly spy', thundered that it was 'ingenious if slightly odd to pitchfork so important an event into a school children's meeting', hence preventing other interested parties from seeing what was going on. How did such secrecy assist Bannister? Perhaps he had the four-minute mile in mind. However, immediately after the race he admitted that he was greatly relieved that he had not run under four-minutes in such bizarre conditions. Even so, P.W. Green, though not a particular admirer of Bannister's general approach, predicted with a high degree of prescience that the first four-minute mile would be run in this kind of event but, he added, 'such races have little benefit as experience for running in top class fields'. What's more, he did not rate Bannister's chances of winning a world-class race.

Although, as the history of mile racing has shown, pacemakers were *de rigeur*, the BAAB was getting sniffy about such performances. A few weeks after the secret mile, the Board issued a statement that they could not recognise the performance as a record, did not even consider the event as a *bona fide* competition, and did not 'regard individual record attempts as in the best interest of athletics as a whole'. It was a good job that he had not run sub-four. But Bannister now realised how close to the four-minute mile he was and in the US Santee only managed 4m. 7.6s. The race was still on.

Throughout the early 1950s, Bannister had to maintain surveillance of those other runners who threatened to beat him to the four-minute milepost. Such a 'race' was intercontinental in character. It was a race where the contestants competed with each other at a distance – of many thousands of miles. As meticulous as ever, Bannister monitored their tactics and their times. He was aided in doing this through his close friendship with an enthusiastic but odd duo, the aforementioned McWhirter twins. Norris and Ross were former Marlborough public schoolboys and ex-Oxford men who would later establish the hugely successful *Guinness Book of Records*. Norris, more ignominiously, also was to host the BBC children's show, *Record Breakers*. In the 1970s Ross was a co-founder of a right wing organisation called the Freedom Association. He and Norris were close friends of Dowager Lady Jane Birdwood, a socialite whose obituary in the *Daily Telegraph* described her as 'a prominent proponent of racialist ideas' and a practitioner of flagrant antisemitism. She was a one time supporter of the British National Party and helped Ross found a far-right, but short-lived, magazine. He was murdered in 1975 by an IRA gunman. Whether the McWhirters' political leanings affected Roger Bannister is uncertain, though his conservative views were later to become pretty evident.

More to the point is the McWhirters' *Athletics World* that ran from 1952 to 1957. Highly informative, well-written but heavily quantitative, it often carried lists of athletes' performances and showed athletic progress by the use of graphs and statistical trends. In its early years it was printed from a typewritten manuscript but provided the serious athlete with monthly injections of information. Roger Bannister was a subscriber. He needed to survey the world scene for potential rivals.

There are two final stories to tell about the 1953 athletics season. One of the most wintry track events in British athletics history took place at Motspur Park on 19 December. Don Macmillan, Bannister's pacemaker at that venue earlier in the year, had not qualified for the Australian Empire Games team. In an attempt to get a decent time before the end of the year a plan was hatched for some of Britain's best runners to aid Macmillan in a paced attempt. Bannister felt that he should reciprocate for Macmillan's sterling effort earlier. The race was dubbed the 'Macmillan Mile' and in the press there was even talk of some sort of record. As it happened, only Bannister and Macmillan actually made the starting line. Bannister ran with the Australian for three laps and then dropped out. Macmillan finished in 4m. 15.6s – outside the qualifying standard. The 'race' was met with an appropriately frosty response. *Athletics Weekly* stated that 'fortunately it will soon be forgotten for the sport cannot afford such bad publicity'.

From a running point of view, Macmillan would have been better off in Australia. His compatriot, John Landy had also run an end of the year mile. On 12 December, in perfect conditions in Melbourne, in a race that featured only four runners (only two finished), Landy had run a new personal best of 4m. 2s. This matched Bannister's best time but the difference between the two results was that Landy had led from start to finish. Even so, he was disappointed. He likened the two seconds needed to get to four minutes to a 'cement wall'. Five weeks later he had another try for the world record. In front of a 25,000 crowd he ran yet another fast time, 4m. 2.3s; 1954 had started with a bang. It was to continue with an explosion.

4

6 MAY 1954

With his Oxbridge chums, Chataway and Brasher, Bannister had planned to make an early season attempt on the four-minute mile. Driven by ambition, Bannister wanted it before anyone else could grab it. The time and the method had been planned in November 1953, aided by the presence of Franz Stampfl, the newly appointed OUAC coach. He seems to have especially helped Chataway and Brasher but Bannister claimed that the ex-Austrian also aided him 'tremendously' in the broader plan as to how the division of labour would be apportioned with his Achilles colleagues.

The McWhirter twins, in the January 1954 issue of *Athletics World*, had flagged 6 May as one of the year's crucial dates. There were also the Australian Championships in Sydney on 11 February and the Penn Relays in Philadelphia on 17 April. Then there was the OUAC *versus* AAA match at Oxford on 6 May. It was in this event, a year earlier, that Bannister had broken the British record. Other dates and places followed in the McWhirters' list. If the record had not been broken by 6 May there would be the chance at other big meets in the US or UK. *Aficionados* would add that there were also the still, summer nights in the Nordic lands of Nurmi and Hägg where fast times seemed inevitable. It was well known to track fans, therefore, that if the races in Sydney and Philadelphia failed to produce a record, Oxford was next on the list.

Again, the race was on. In March Gunder Hägg had forecast that Bannister would get the four-minute mile first: 'He has brains', the world record holder announced, 'and doesn't over-train the way most runners do. You don't see Bannister burning himself out'. Having only run 4m. 5.6s on the rain-soaked grass of the Sydney Cricket Ground in the Australian championships, Landy ran 4m. 2.6s, in April at Bendigo, Victoria, the fastest ever mile on a grass track. An ocean and half-a-continent away in Philadelphia, the other protagonist Santee, ran 4m. 3.1s. Two of the year's big meets had come and gone: Hägg's record remained intact. But if Landy could run that fast on grass, how fast could he run on the magical tracks of Stockholm, Gothenburg, Helsinki or Turku, regarded as being among the fastest in the world? Such possibilities were in Bannister's mind as he prepared for the annual meeting at Iffley Road, a track which he had been instrumental in re-constructing, almost a second home. Having created the track, he now set out to create the record.

Essential to the four-minute project was the capability of the pacemakers. In April, as Landy was running close to the record in Australia, Stampfl and Bannister were checking out the prospects of Brasher taking him through two-and-a-half laps at world record pace. At a municipal cinder track, in an industrial area at Alperton, near Wembley, the home track of Thames Valley Harriers, Brasher was put through his paces in a half-mile time trial. He recorded 1m. 56.7s, rated good enough for his Oxford duties the following month. Such checking of detail further exemplifies Bannister's (and Stampfl's) seriousness. Chataway, with his strength as a three-miler and his pace-making experience, presented no doubts.

Bannister had trained hard all winter and in the three weeks before the May attempt he had applied himself to high quality training sessions of interval running. In mid-April he ran seven separate half-miles with three minutes rest between each run. He had run a solo half-mile in 1m. 53s; in another session ten separate quarter-miles were run in an average time of 58.9s; in another, a three-quarter mile in 3m. 14s and another in 3m. 8.6s with eight minutes recovery between each. On 28 April he had run another pre-race three-quarters of a mile on his own in 2m. 59.9s in a high wind. Three people were there to witness it. He then took five days rest until the day of the race. He felt he was ready but was not overconfident.

In his usual meticulous way, Bannister attended to even the tiniest of details in the days that preceded the event. He had tried using a variety of track shoes, including the new (to Britain) German-made 'shoes with three stripes' – slogan and trade mark of the Adidas shoe company, now beginning to export their shoes throughout western Europe. However, for the 6 May race he chose to have his shoes hand-made on the instructions of a fell-walker, a Mancunian admirer named Eustace Thomas. He had visited Bannister in London and together they made changes that would reduce the weight of his shoes from six to four ounces, about the weight of a moderate bag of sweets. He was well aware, in his own words, that this 'saving in weight might well mean the difference between success and failure'. He had also sharpened his spikes on a laboratory grindstone, as if to make him faster. He applied graphite to the soles in order to avoid dirt or cinders from the track becoming attached and adding extra weight. There was nothing 'amateur' (nor particularly 'gentlemanly' – 'workmanlike' would be a better term) about such a technical approach and today's sports commentators would probably call such preparation and attention to detail a sign of the consummate 'professional'.

GETTING SET

It has been said that England has no climate, only weather. Early May weather in England cannot be predicted. It could be snowing or it could be almost scorching. The forecast for the city of Oxford on 6 May

1954 was for blustery showers. Bannister, now based in London as a postgraduate medical student at St Mary's Hospital, made the morning trip from Paddington to Oxford by train. Also on the train was Stampfl. His relation to Bannister remains unclear. Bannister's view is that he was less a coach and more an advisor, though Stampfl may have felt differently. Bannister's line has been that he was prepared to listen to advice but ultimately he was his own man. That was the great thing about running. If you had no obligations to a coach, there was only one person to blame if things went wrong.

Stampfl claimed that his major achievement was to get Chataway and Brasher fit enough for them to pace Bannister for the first three laps of the record attempt. He claimed that the three of them 'sat down and organised the entire approach to the first four-minute mile'. Brasher agreed that Stampfl was the major strategist for the record result. In his book (*First Four Minutes*), however, Bannister seems to have downplayed Stampfl's role but, according to the American athletics writer Kenny Moore, this need not be seen as a terminological inexactitude. According to Moore, Bannister wrote the dream instead of the reality. Nevertheless, later he did acknowledge that Stampfl, through his counsel if not his coaching, had often helped him 'to defeat formidable opponents on the track'. According to one of his subsequent trainees, he 'was dictatorial' and 'adamant in his views', his dictum being 'Don't worry, it's only pain'.

Stampfl felt that during the journey to Oxford, Bannister 'was nervous and kept talking about why it [the record] wouldn't be possible'. The weather, wet and windy, looked too inclement. However, Stampfl argued that because of his preparation he was fit enough to run 3m. 56s so if there was some wind or rain it wouldn't matter too much as he could still run under four minutes. Of course, 3m. 59.9s would not be good enough since the official policy of 'rounding up' the result to 'exactly' four minutes would have been anticlimactic. He may never have another chance. He had planned this for months. He had to do it that evening; it was now or never. Whether Stampfl's input was 'coaching' or not is debateable. 'Prodding' might be a better word.

One thing that an Oxford education does is that it establishes good networks, friends of friends, it's who you know, always a place to put your head down, a port in every storm. Having alighted from his train, Bannister was met by David 'Charles' Wenden, a former half-miler, Oxford 'blue', holder of the Military Cross and one of his early running colleagues. Wenden would later become the college bursar at both St Catherine's and All Souls. Wenden drove Bannister down to Iffley Road where the wind seemed to be gale force. The two friends walked round the deserted track. A record attempt seemed out of the question. Even so, Bannister tried out the two pairs of spikes he had brought with him but this did not aid him in making a decision. However, there was still six hours to go. The British record holder for the mile had lunch at Charles and Eileen Wenden's comfortable home, dining on ham salad and, appropriately given the possible tension surrounding the event, prunes. Relaxing after lunch by playing with Wenden's children, Felicity and Sally, he managed to forget his nervousness by observing domestic routines. He called on Chataway and together they mulled over the Oxford weather. With News of the World journalist and old-time British miler, Joe Binks, they set off for the track, arriving at the 90-year-old changing rooms at five o'clock, the starting time of the meeting and an hour before the scheduled start of the mile.

The crowd of somewhere between 1,000 and 2,000 was made up of the usual university types with their college scarves and tweed jackets. But Iffley Road was no White City Stadium and it was possible to see the race from the three and four storey villas across the road. It might have been just possible to get a glimpse of it by peeping over the Iffley Road fence. Overcoats, gloves and scarves, light brown duffel coats, trilbies and cloth caps, rather than shirt-sleeves, were the dress order of the day. Unknown to the highly-strung young star of British miling, Alice and Ralph Bannister were there too, proud no doubt but not flaunting their son's prowess. Pipe-smoking dons mixed and mingled with men with clipboards who would do the officiating. Cambridge alumnus and long-term member of the Achilles Club, Harold Abrahams, was there as one of the timekeepers.

The BBC knew about the possibility of a fast time only because Norris McWhirter had alerted them to the possibility a couple of days before. One cameraman and his assistant had turned up with the appropriate outdoor equipment to televise the event. If a world record was set it would be shown on their evening sports review. The camera was sited in the middle of the arena (rather than outside the track as is common today). The usual journalists, from hacks like Desmond Hackett of the *Daily Express* to the more cerebral Larry Montague of the *Manchester Guardian* were in attendance, as were the photographers who supplied the sports magazines and popular press with their images. Hardly surprising, the Oxford graduates, the McWhirter twins, were there to record the event. Indeed, Norris was not only the event's announcer but had also been chosen to represent the AAA in the sprint relay! Ross was the lone unofficial timekeeper at the 1,500 metres mark. Spectators stood on the grassy bank surrounding the track. Others filled the grandstand and an unusually large number of people occupied the field area inside the track. Track-suited athletes from other events, eager to get a close-up view, television technicians from the BBC with microphones in hand, should an interview with the winner be needed, and officials and timekeepers, lap counters and so on, made the place look less clinical than the performance, which, in fact, it was. Compared with events at the White City Stadium it all seemed pretty disorganised. Staid handclapping greeted the shot-putters and high-jumpers.

The question remained: would the physical environment thwart the record attempt? The weather couldn't be totally neutralised but there was at least a chance that the clouds wouldn't open and the wind might still drop. Amid the grey clouds there was an occasional hint of blue. Stampfl urged Bannister to warm up and then make the decision whether to go for it or not. Warmed and supple, the time was 5.45 p.m. and a decision had to be made. Bannister said 'no'; the wind was impossibly inhospitable; the Union flag was flying at 90 degrees to the mast, straining at the halyards, of the church of St John the Evangelist, the tower of which was clearly visible from the track. Stampfl later recalled that Bannister was in a 'blue mood' and initially 'refused to run' in such conditions. Brasher said 'yes' and Chataway couldn't care less. Rumour has it that Stampfl kept delaying the start. The runners carried on doing a few strides and with five minutes to go, the wind suddenly dropped. It couldn't have been scripted better. Bannister was persuaded. The runners donned their spiked shoes and the race – or more accurately, the record attempt – was on.

A SUCCESSFUL EXPERIMENT

Six runners toed the starting line. Roger Bannister, Chris Chataway, Chris Brasher and Tom Hulatt, the northern champion, represented the AAA and the American Rhodes theological scholar George Dole and future international Alan Gordon represented the university. A third Oxford runner, T.J. Miller, was in the programme but did not appear at the starting line. There have been two suggested reasons: he either dropped out at the last minute or was not told that he was supposed to be competing. As the McWhirters said in their race report, he is probably still kicking himself. Apart from Bannister, none of the others could be said to be world-class milers. They were solid, high-quality runners at other distances, especially Chataway who, later in the year, would briefly become world record holder for 5,000 metres, beating Vladimir Kuts in the process. And Brasher was the only one of the three *compadres* to become an Olympic champion – in the steeplechase in 1956. Even so, nobody but Bannister was going to win this race; the question was how long he would take to do it. Yes, on paper it was a team race between the university and the AAA but in reality it was a planned attempt on the world record, a race against time, by Bannister's hand-picked team.

It seems that the universities of Oxford and Cambridge had been well known for their athletes' use of pacemaking for many years. According to the Abrahams brothers in 1928, pacemaking is 'mainly seen in "Varsity racing" when record attempts are being made' (italics added). The job of the pacemaker was traditionally to set the optimal pace for the 'first string' runner. So on 6 May 1954 it was a team effort with each runner having a distinct role, a classic division of labour in the best industrial tradition. The event focused much more on the pace than the race. The running track was both an assembly line and a laboratory for a scientific experiment, the testing of the model mile – four minutes flat: no more and hopefully a little less.

Bannister led the experiment. Brasher and Chataway were his research assistants, the other runners mere students of the event, watching it unfold from afar. Indeed, according to Tom Hulatt, Bannister told him that he should avoid the three members involved in the experiment and run his own race. In other words, he should keep out of their way. As members of the team, Chataway and Brasher were not sacrificing anything themselves. It was not as if they were of the same standard as Bannister. There was nothing chivalric about their participation. They, like Hulatt, knew their place. Now it was up to other factors to deter- mine if the experiment would be successful. The plan was for Brasher to lead for at least two laps; Chataway would take on the crucial third quarter and then, as in the same meet the previous year, Bannister would do the rest, hopefully helped by the absence of the prevailing wind and the presence of a vociferous home crowd.

The Iffley Road crowd waited silently. The starter raised his pistol but Brasher made a false start in his excitement to get going: more tension. For the second time of asking the starter performed his ritual task. They were off, Brasher straight into the lead as planned. Bannister felt easy. Halfway round the first lap, feeling that his lightweight spikes made him run on air, he called to Brasher to go faster, but the Cambridge-educated steeplechaser maintained his discipline rather than increased his speed. Anyway, the first furlong was the fastest of the race. Already it was a three-man experiment, or exhibition. There was no crowd of runners to clutter things up. Of necessity the other three participants were involved in what was effectively, another event. At 440 yards the announcer called out the first-lap time: 57.4s. This was fast but not too fast: not as fast as Henry Eriksson had run (56s) when pacing Hägg to his world record in 1942.

Brasher continued his job for the second lap (Figure 4.1). Slowing down but still on schedule, the halfway mark was reached in 1m. 58s. Now the crowd began to get excited: a record was on the cards. With about 600 yards to go Chataway took over and, supported by the growing noise of the crowd ended the third lap in 3m. 0.4s. He held the lead for another 30 yards or so before the final furlong, at which point Bannister strode past him. Ross McWhirter, standing with stopwatch in hand at the 1,500 metres point, stopped his watch at

Figure 4.1 Division of labour: Brasher (right) and Chataway (left) assisting Bannister during the four-minute mile, Iffley Road, Oxford, 6 May 1954 (*The Oxford Mail*)

3m. 43s – equal (unofficially) to the world record held jointly by the two Swedes, Hägg and Strand and the German, Lueg. The mile record still lay in the balance. Bannister had only equalled the metric record; and he could still break the mile record but be outside four minutes. After all, the pace had hardly been perfect. He drove himself without mercy towards the haven of the finishing tape. His elegant stride displayed the beauty of the human body but his face exhibited fatigue and pain. Photographers recorded him crossing the line but the large crowd on the infield meant that many of the resulting prints were of poor quality. Even the film camera had problems with the crowds and could only record the finish from the side!

Bannister saw the tape coming. His chest broke it with his head thrown back, face contorted, eyes closed and mouth open, gasping for breath. The cheering was now deafening. Charles Wenden, an official at the meeting, clutched his clipboard in one hand and buried his face in the other, unsure of the outcome. Norris McWhirter had spent years watching track races and claimed to have an uncanny knack of being able to watch the finish with one eye and his stopwatch with the other; he felt that Bannister had done it. The spectators who had timed the race with their own pocket watches, even stopwatches, were not too sure about the record either. It required an AAA certificated timekeeper for a record to be accepted and wristwatches were risky when timing to the nearest second. Chataway completed the race some 40 yards behind, still running hard, and achieving a personal best time of 4m. 7.2s. Further behind was Hulatt, still running at a respectable pace, and way back was Brasher. The other two runners were unable to complete the race, as spectators who couldn't wait to congratulate their hero swamped the track. But the official result had yet to be announced.

Bannister had collapsed, exhausted: his pulse rate was taken; it was 155. At rest it was between 40 and 50 and he had to wait three hours before it returned to normal. His colour vision was nil. Supported by Stampfl he was led away to recover, giving the distinct impression that he had exhausted his available energy just as he broke the tape, A. V. Hill's ideal method, the perfect organisation of exhaustion. The timekeepers, experienced men in the timing of talent (or what the German cultural theorist, Walter Benjamin, thought was modernity *par excellence* – the measuring of the human being against an apparatus), were in a huddle, poring over their timepieces. Three watches had been stopped at the same time (only the second time in half-a-century that there had been such agreement on the time of a world mile record). The result could now be written down and passed to Norris McWhirter whose job it was to announce it officially. Wishing to do things properly, as if giving a speech at a college high table, and trying to be as unemotional as possible, but at the same time teasing the crowd with what Garry Whannel read as a 'well-judged piece of theatre', he adopted what he called the 'crescendo-suspense' approach. His exact words were:

> Ladies and gentlemen, here is the result of event number nine, the one mile: first, number 41, R.G. Bannister, of the Amateur Athletics Association and formerly of Exeter and Merton Colleges, with a time which is a new meeting and track record and which subject to ratification will be a new English Native, British (National), British (All-comers), European, British Empire and World Record. The time is *three* (and lost in the roar were the words) *minutes fifty-nine point four seconds*.

The four-minute mile was no longer a dream. Bannister had not only broken through a prison of measured time, his time had broken Hägg's record by two seconds, the biggest improvement on a world mile record since Nurmi. His exhaustion had gone and with his friends he 'scampered round the track in a burst of spontaneous joy'.

The crowd hardly went berserk but certainly displayed more than normal English reserve – 'intelligent enthusiasm' as *The Times* athletics correspondent put it. It was not quite polite applause but a hugely enjoyable combination of cheering and shouting. Spectators had seen something akin to Harry Houdini's escapology, witnessing a new way in which the human body could be tested, or seeing what a human being could willingly do to his own slender and vulnerable body. During the race they had been unaware of whether Bannister would succeed or fail – whether he could escape the prison of measured time or remain stuck on the wrong side of the barrier. For some, it could have even had the appearance of a stunt: there was no trick – or if there was, it couldn't be seen.

Ross McWhirter conferred and congratulated him. Other friends, autograph hunters, BBC interviewers, and reporters accosted the new record holder. His interview, as recorded by the BBC, was modest. He said that he was absolutely overwhelmed and delighted and that it was a great surprise to him that he was able to do it on the day. He thought he was very lucky. The Oxford understatement (dare one say false modesty?) was still there; if he was successful it was not because of science, training and pacing but because of luck. Photographs were taken of the famous threesome with Stampfl getting into the act to pose with them too. Some BAAB officials asked Brasher and Chataway whether they had tried to win the race (i.e. making it a 'legitimate' competition) to which they replied, 'Yes, of course'. Brasher was cheeky enough to say that he had dreamed of winning himself. Bannister went over to thank Walter Norris, the venerable Iffley Road groundsman, whose job it had been to prepare and tend the track, to turn it from nature into culture. It took nearly half-an-hour for the athletics meeting to restart.

The three-man team washed and changed and returned to central Oxford where, in Vincent's, a posh drinking club for Oxford sportsmen whose membership was by election, they refreshed themselves. Bannister shunned champagne and had a glass of salted water and a shandy. The BBC, anxious to get Bannister interviewed, had a fast car waiting to whisk him to Lime Grove Studios where, on the popular 'Sportsnight' programme fronted by the redoubtable Peter Dimmock, he again responded modestly to his stellar achievement. He said that, while feeling bewildered, the four-minute was not all that important to him and that it was winning races against international competition that mattered. Neither comment had been supported by his career thus far. He also promoted the 'gentleman amateur' line that running was still a hobby for him. But beneath the façade there was exuberance that, with Bannister's social background and his cultural capital, he could readily repress. As Gordon Pirie was to say of him later, he seemed to be always holding back his emotions. But he felt he had now wiped out the defeat (and the disgrace according to some of the British press) in the Olympic final.

In fact, they were two quite different events. The Helsinki Olympic final was a race; the Oxford experiment was a pace. He would have to prove his racing ability later in the year, perhaps in the Empire Games in Canada or in the European 1,500 metres championship in Switzerland where an Olympic quality field would be assembled.

The BBC interview completed, there was now time to meet up with Brasher, Chataway and three female friends. They adjourned for celebrations to a nightclub in the West End. The club officially closed at 3.30 a.m. but the band stayed on to play for the new world record holder who, at 5.00 was given the microphone and crooned 'Time on my hands'. The party ended half an hour later and, at 6.45 a.m. Bannister took two hour's sleep in Brasher's Highgate home. Back at St Mary's, they had hoisted the Union Jack. Like the same flag on Everest, it symbolised a national achievement.

5

AFTER THE EVENT

On the morning of 7 May at St Mary's Hospital, Bannister's colleagues hoisted him on to their shoulders in a triumphal, heroic pose for the press. The UK news media carried massive coverage of the four-minute mile. The event was front page – indeed, headline – news in most British newspapers. The reports of the race, including that in the *New York Times*, invariably featured a large photograph of Bannister breasting the tape. As Andrew Blake has noted, this 'crossover' of sport from back page to front page (except, in those days, *The Times*, of course), made the drama of the four-minute mile a truly public event, for a time displacing the routine stories of economics and politics. The May issue of the McWhirters' *Athletics World*, was unsurprisingly congratulatory. It included the most detailed report of the race that exists and a photograph of Bannister and Chataway, smiling at each other after the race. Dispensing with the comic convention of balloons coming out of the respective mouths, the caption read: 'Thanks Chris', 'Good show Roger'.

Harold Abrahams, whose numerous activities included that of a BBC broadcaster, spoke on the radio programme 'Home and Abroad'. He stated that the record caused him 'more emotional disturbance' than any event he had ever seen in 40 years of association with track and field athletics. More emotion had been disturbed, therefore, than on the 'perfect race' run by Jack Lovelock at the Berlin Olympics. Abrahams continued: 'Bannister richly deserved the record since no man could have possibly *trained harder*' (italics added). And elsewhere, the accolades flowed freely. The Olympic champion, Joseph Barthel congratulated Bannister with the words, 'hard work pays'. He, like Abrahams, did not read Bannister as a light trainer. Nor was he seen as a slacker in the USA. The *New York Times* remarked that 'his approach to running is coldly scientific'. On the other hand, a well-known athletics coach, Brutus Hamilton, partly slipping into romantic, 'Merrie England' mode, said, 'I'm glad Roger did it. The lad is a real amateur [more on this later]. He runs only because he loves to run. And he prepares himself well'. Ken Doherty went further. Writing in *Scholastic Coach* he felt that Bannister's 'significance to sport lies in the fact that he is the *perfect amateur* and still beats the world' (italics added). The amateur imagery of the Americans' assessments rested somewhat uneasily with the talk of 'coldly scientific' hard training but there was no doubt that the first four-minute mile generated a positive response. Veteran reporter Arthur Daley saw Bannister's record as 'trackdom's Holy Grail'. From an athletic, but also hyperbolic, standpoint, he added that 'this is as historic as the breaking of the sound barrier'.

NEGATIVE FEEDBACK

Praise for the four-minute mile was paralleled by less euphoric views. *Athletics Weekly*, for several decades the main voice serving British athletics fans, editorialised about the event and provided a report on it. Here a more critical voice was heard, much less eulogistic than the national press and the Oxford group (i.e. the McWhirters) which had been, more or less, part of the event. '*AW*' was the athletes' magazine and while the editor certainly congratulated the new world record holder he tempered his praise with a sense of reserve and even negation.

Drawing on earlier criticism, he sombrely stated that 'He [Bannister] has yet to win a race against world-class opposition and running in cut-throat competition is very different to running in a race where one's competition is so helpful'. As I indicated earlier, *Athletics Weekly* carried a vigorous letters column. However, the number of letters printed about Bannister and the four-minute mile was relatively small and barely extended beyond the issue published the week after the event. This, of course, may have reflected the possibility that only a small number of letters about the four-minute mile were submitted. But even if this was the case there were certainly more letters published a year earlier on the question of whether athletics meetings should take place on Sundays, and likewise, concerning Bannister's paltry response to the magazine's questionnaire.

One of the longest and strongest letters followed the line taken by the editor. It was far from unqualified praise. Yes, it was a great performance but things should be kept in perspective: 'Athletics should be a competitive sport, and that means competition against opponents, not merely against the clock'. Bannister should undertake more racing and training and being a medical student was no excuse: 'You can't say you're the best miler until you've proved it in competition, Roger'. And Wooderson and Pirie had done far more for British athletics than Bannister had. Was this British self-loathing or an anti-Achilles tendency? It certainly saw Bannister in a less heroic light than would be portrayed decades later. And even his admirer, Harold Abrahams, was careful to point out that 'we should be on our guard against making sport too much of a stunt'. The stopwatch should not matter more than the victory. It would have been easy to see how this kind of event might turn out if put in the hands of a sports entrepreneur. Such an exhibition invited gimmicks, razzmatazz and showbiz.

Nor was overseas reaction necessarily euphoric. In Australia, the reception was mixed. The leader comment in the *Sydney Morning Herald* reflected a stiff upper lip: 'Australians may be excused for wishing that the four-minute mile had fallen to Landy … but there is great consolation in the fact that the honour belongs, none the less, to the British Commonwealth'. However, there was a minor sting in the tail: 'But breaking 3.59 will be always seen, *quite unreasonably*, a lesser feat than breaking 4.00' (emphasis added). This comment implied that when, inevitably, Landy broke Bannister's record it would be of at least equal, if not greater, worth, even if not recognised by the British as such. A couple of days after the record run *The Age* athletics writer, Bruce Welch, noted that Landy had been handicapped from breaking the record 'by conditions, lack of competition and expert guidance'.

Some of the Australian press, and some athletes, took a different line that focused more on Bannister's approach. The Oxford event was said to be 'overorganised', too planned, not a proper race. One particularly strident criticism came from the Aussie correspondent of *Athletics World*, J.H. Galli. He observed that Landy (through Australian eyes, the epitome of the amateur sportsman) 'would never have been a party to such a schemed "race" as Bannister employed'. He said repeatedly that he 'wanted to do it (the four-minute mile) "fair dinkum" '. More recently Landy himself has recalled: 'I wouldn't have done it that way myself, using a pacesetter. I didn't want to be part of something questionable, which is how pacesetting was seen at that time'. In short, Bannister was read as having benefitted from unfair assistance. Indeed, he acknowledged that he 'could not have done it without Chataway and Brasher' who played the role of 'ghost runners'. The four-minute mile was paced, not raced. So *did* Bannister cheat? Did he have an unfair advantage? And who 'owned' the record? Bannister alone? Perhaps, as in ghost-written books, the first four-minute mile should be recorded as having been undertaken by 'Roger Bannister *with* Chris Brasher and Chris Chataway'.

That uncharitable genius, Paavo Nurmi, was, as might be expected, curt and to the point: 'There's nothing unusual about a four-minute mile', he said. 'It's only a question of intensified training': talk about being damned by faint praise. His compatriot, Denis Johansson, was even more more scathing. 'What's Bannister done?', he asked, followed by his answer: 'Third in a European 800 metres championship' (four years earlier).

Several 'experts' felt that the record would soon be broken, Santee and Landy being the obvious favourites. Now Bannister had done it, several US commentators thought it would become commonplace – and Bannister felt the same. Even the 1948 and 1952 Olympic 800 metres champion Mal Whitfield, who had no miling credentials and who had failed to get anywhere near four minutes on a mile-long boardwalk in Atlantic City, New Jersey, stated that he could run 3m. 56.5s. The US coach Payton Jordan predicted that 'it's only a matter of time until they get the record down to 3m. 55s'. In fact, it took only four years but these observations verged on negation, implying that the four-minute mile was not that much of an achievement after all.

The record had been set but would it be ratified? Given the BAAB's earlier statement about pacemaking and events being non-competitive there was the possibility that the first four-minute mile would be treated with the same disdain as the 'secret' mile at Motspur Park. After all, as the critics pointed out, the 6 May race had been hardly competitive; it had certainly been a record attempt and there was no way of denying that pacemakers were involved. But the fact that it was a bona fide competition legitimised things and all was well. Brasher and Chataway had finished the 'race' and contributed to the scoring in the match of which it was part. Although this was irrelevant to the record it was central to its acceptance. The record was quickly ratified and submitted to the IAAF as a world record. It was approved as a world record on 15 June – before anyone got the chance to break it.

The pacemaking debate resurfaced in 1956 when it was ruled by the BAAB that a record would not be passed if a runner had received any 'unfair assistance' from pacemakers 'apparently designed to assist him to achieve a record'. Bannister, writing in the Sunday Times, admitted that if this rule had been in force in May 1954, his record would have been outlawed. He also stated that if the rule was applied internationally, Landy's subsequent world record would have been ruled out for being advertised as a planned record attempt. The BAAB rule proved impossible to apply as the notion of an 'unfair' pacemaker could not be satisfactorily defined. In any case, the practice had a long pedigree and today, for better or worse, pacemaking is normal in most big athletics events.

Despite the downplaying of Bannister's effort by some observers he was, on the day after the race, hot property. The press was after him and he rushed off to that reliable bolt-hole, the Wenden's home in Oxford where he let the worst of the adulation subside. But, just over a week after the record, he undertook a visit to the USA. A television producer had approached the British Information Services with the invitation. The Foreign Office – seeing the visit as a means of promoting Anglo–American relations – was very happy to ask Bannister who readily accepted, though he viewed it as 'the strangest of missions'. He was hugely popular and took part in various media events but no races. He was offered a trophy said to be worth $300 but, as according to the rules of amateur athletics the value of a prize should have been no more than £12, he had to accept a cheap replica in its place! The question of amateur status seemed to be pervasive. Among the questions he was asked was whether he would be knighted. He was stunned by the question but in 1974 he was, indeed, made a knight of the realm. By then he was a neurologist and had been the first chairman of the Sports Council. But did he ever wonder how much the four-minute mile had contributed to his knighthood?

Nobody in Britain had sensed his amateur status was at risk until it was realised that he had been asked to appear on a television show sponsored by the R.J. Reynold's Tobacco Company. This could be seen as a way of exploiting Bannister's reputation and there was also the question of whether there would be a fee paid for his appearance. Any fees, it had been agreed, would be paid to charities. The question of amateur status led the Foreign Office to decide that it would be best if he didn't appear on that particular programme.

It may be of passing interest to record that the question of the arrangements for Bannister's visit was raised in the House of Commons.

The Secretary of State for Foreign Affairs, Selwyn Lloyd, was keen to point out that Her Majesty's Government had assumed full financial responsibility for the visit. The government rated the visit a great success but, yet again, Roger Bannister had been involved in a mini-controversy.

THE 46-DAY RECORD

But back to the world of sport: who would be next world record holder? How long would it take for the record to be broken? In fact, it would be less than two months. Bannister had easily won the so-called 'race' at Oxford; he had won the race to the world record; he had beaten Santee and Landy to the four-minute mile. But the new record simply represented a new target. Bannister himself, in a moment of exuberance or weakness, said he now felt he could run 3m. 56s, perhaps recalling an earlier comment that the wind on 6 May 'cut me down by two or three seconds'.

On 6 June in California, at the Compton Invitational track fest, Wes Santee, the crew-cut Kansan, tried to make actions speak louder than words and made a serious attempt to reach the new record-horizon. In atypically cool and windy weather Santee ran the second fastest mile ever, 4m. 0.6s but *en route* broke Hägg's world 1,500 metres record with a new mark of 3m. 42.8s. These times were the fastest he would ever run. He was a world record holder, the American star, the pride of Kansas, successor to the previous Kansas giant, Glenn Cunningham, and attracted huge publicity. But there were financial abuses – he had accepted 'excess expenses' (at least the dollar equivalent of £540) and at 23 years of age he was kicked out of the amateur ranks by the stringent American Athletic Union. He sued the AAU but lost the suit.

It was John Landy, who had been recording such consistently fast times in Australia, who was to break Bannister's record. A racing tour of Sweden and Finland had been arranged for him. First stop was on 21 May, in Turku, south-west Finland and home of Paavo Nurmi, whose statue stands just outside the stadium. A race over one mile had been arranged with pacemakers on hand, one being Denis Johansson. The race started and the assigned pacemaker took the lead but after 150 metres Landy would have none of it and went ahead, moving like a half-miler: first lap 56.5s; the half-mile 1m. 55.8s. Landy was a dedicated front-runner and had once said that he would rather lose a mile in 3m. 58s than win one in 4m. 10s. He wanted speed more than victory. Landy appeared to be flowing on what was regarded as one of the fastest tracks in the world. But although the pace was hot the weather was cool and windy. Running in splendid isolation he was forced to slow down but even so finished in 4m. 1.6s, the best part of 80 metres in front of two top Finnish athletes.

Landy's next race was at Stockholm where the temperature was only 9° C and the track was described as 'heavy'. Yet, by a coincidence, he won in exactly the same time as in his Scandinavian debut, though arriving at the time via a different tactical route. As an experiment he followed the pacemakers with a restrained first half of 1m. 59.7s. Alone for the second half of the race, he finished with an excellent sprint even though there was no opposition in sight. Two lower key races followed this, both of which he won easily. But what about the four-minute mile that his Australian fans were sure he could run? Was Landy still stuck in the 4m.1s/4m.2s groove? Were his Nordic performances really any better than his Aussie efforts? Was there anything in Landy's claim that his home-based results were retarded by the poor quality of Australia's running tracks? Or was it a case that, as the unorthodox Aussie, Percy Cerutty, suggested, Landy was too soft and unprepared to drive himself with more punishing efforts?

On 21 June he made his way back to Turku where the temperature was a much more congenial 25° C, with clear air and setting sun, the kind of Nordic evening which many athletes dream about and which has become the mythical ideal for fast running; 8,000 fans turned up at the municipal stadium. As at Oxford there were six starters. As at Oxford there was Chris Chataway who reckoned that it was the best day he had ever known for running. The field was completed by four

Finns, among them Olavi Vuorisalo who would later become a world record breaker in the 1,500 metres. As usual, a pacemaker was laid on and, again unusually restrained, Landy held himself back for the first 700 metres. He then cruised smoothly into the lead and passed the half-mile in 1m. 57.9s, inside the world record pace but not so far inside to cause his supporters to panic. But Chataway was only about two or three metres behind, making Landy aware that there was an opponent – but one who was desperately trying to hang on. On the third lap Landy stepped up the pace, opening a ten metre lead. He passed the 1,500 metres point at which, with typically Finnish efficiency, three official timekeepers were stationed, in a smashing world record time of 3m. 41.8s – and found energy to accelerate and maintain his rhythm, sprinting faster than Bannister had at Oxford, to finish in a stunning time of 3m. 57.9s. He crossed the line smiling, with no apparent signs of distress. He readily ran an 'applause lap' (Figure 5.1). Chataway, pacer for Bannister, now found himself the beneficiary of Landy's pace. In the second four-minute mile ever run, the Englishman, though well behind Landy, again recorded a personal best, this time 4m. 4.4s – a great result for a miler, let alone a 5,000 metres specialist.

Now that there were two four-minute milers, one was inevitably compared with the other. Somewhat contrarily, the London *Evening News* sided with Landy, seeming to mirror the views of some British fans and club runners who saw Bannister as a toff. 'Nobody could call Landy's Turku success a fluke. It has been worked for harder than any other mile in history' stated the *News*. 'Landy, of all men, may be said to have driven himself to success' (emphasis added). Some reporters saw Bannister's record as a team effort. Landy's success, however, was read here as his alone. From an Australian perspective it was 'as much a feat of pioneering as the work of our forefathers' showing 'the same indomitable spirit, courage and endurance', claimed a letter to the *Melbourne Age*.

Bannister's record had lasted 46 days; Santee's only 17. The world of track and field was stunned. A professor of physiology at Sydney

Figure 5.1 John Landy, shortly after breaking Bannister's record, Turku, Finland, 21 June, 1954 (author's collection)

University felt that a result of under 3m. 58s indicated that 'we are getting close to the limit', implying that Landy was the ultimate miler. Records that had previously been sacred now became profane but Landy knew that it would not be too long before he would also be relegated to a position among yesterday's men. A year earlier he had said that 'a few years and you're just a name in a list of performances'. There is no esteem in reaching the levels of past runners. That's the problem with speeding up. Associated with it is a relative slowing down. What was once seen as fast is now ordinary.

Another Australian perspective on Bannister, unreported to British fans, alludes to his reaction to Landy's new record. While Bannister publicly congratulated his record-breaker, it was said that he had felt possessive about the world mile record. Additionally, Bannister was said to be surprised about – even to have taken exception to – Chataway going to Finland to race Landy so soon after the Oxford landmark. Landy had also reacted negatively to suggestions that his improvement on Bannister's record was a result of the so-called psychological barrier having been demolished: 'In other words. All thanks to Bannister'.

Away from the track circuit of Scandinavia and in heavy rain at the White City Stadium in the Whitsun 'British Games', Bannister lost a half-mile race to the Czech, Stanislav Jungwirth, against whom he would later compete in Bern. He also offered some kind of reciprocity to Chataway by helping him with some pacemaking in an attempt to break the British two mile record. Bannister, unused to running such a distance on the track, finished the race in a painful seventh place. As a result he suffered sore muscles. He had also, of course, suffered an interruption to his training by the hectic nature of his life following the 6 May epic.

However, on 12 June he trotted around another mile – in 4m. 29s. It was almost a training run, in which he deliberately dead-heated with a fellow medical student and former Oxford cross-country colleague, James Scott-Wilson in the Inter Hospitals' championships. To complete a light (hearted) training session he also won the half-mile in just under two minutes. More seriously, Bannister's Oxford success had attracted a large crowd to the White City Stadium for the 1954 AAA championships. They were hoping for another four-minute mile but, though winning, his final time was 'only' 4m. 7.6s. Lost on many spectators was Bannister's fantastic last quarter-mile, timed at 53.8s. It was the fastest ever last lap recorded in the history of the mile race. This must have given him confidence for the serious business that would start in August.

For athletics fans, 1954 was like an athletic Aladdin's cave, a seemingly unending spree of records and races. But the best was yet to come. The month of August would witness, first, the fifth British Empire and Commonwealth Games in Vancouver, British Columbia and later, the European Athletics championships in Bern, Switzerland. Bannister was entered for both. The former matched him against Landy; the latter engaged him with the best runners Europe could offer.

MILE OF THE CENTURY

The Vancouver Empire Games were promoted as the site of either the 'mile of the century', the 'battle of the titans', or the 'miracle mile'. But at the same time the Games were supposed to symbolise the Empire and Commonwealth. Nation would mix and mingle with nation. The common currency of sport would bond people together. At least, that was the theory. Athletes are individuals. Some take sport more seriously than others. Among those who were serious about success in the Vancouver Empire Games was Roger Bannister. In transit at Gander, Newfoundland, many of the English team hung around looking miserable but Bannister's more 'professional' approach, as recalled by Brian Hewson, dictated that he used the time exercising, pacing about, finding inactivity displeasing.

At events like the Empire Games, non-university athletes quickly observed that those from Oxford and Cambridge did everything together, even sitting at separate tables. This was not totally unreasonable as they were friends. But they were widely regarded as snobs. Bannister was sometimes seen in the same way. Derek Ibbotson, like Bannister a former grammar school boy and former world mile record holder, said that he and Bannister had nothing in common except that they could each run a fast mile. Unlike Ibbotson, Bannister was hardly an 'athlete's athlete', seldom seen with any but his own circle of friends, inevitably including Chataway, apparently aloof or shy. He was more remembered for his singleness of purpose, a quality that was reflected in the way he and Chataway successfully avoided the army of journalists and fans who had descended on Vancouver. According to Brian Hewson, they simply misled the journalists by telling them that they would be training at one place but then turning up at another. Hewson recalled that Landy, on the other hand, was happy to train in public.

The Empire Games mile of 1954 was, of course, always going to be a two-man race. Bannister had the reputation of having the best finishing sprint of any miler; Landy was the greatest pace runner ever seen. It was presented as a contest between speed and stamina. The 6 May race at Oxford was low-key; the one scheduled for Vancouver, 7 August, was high profile. How would the race be run? It was reckoned that if the pace was slow Bannister would probably win by out-sprinting Landy with 150 yards to go – unless the latter set off with a sustained surge from the halfway mark. A world-record pace from the start would severely test Bannister since Landy's stamina had been proved by fast times at 2,000 metres and two miles whilst in Scandinavia.

The mile heats were no problem. In Bannister's heat an Australian set off at a fast pace, hoping to take the sting out of his running and hence give Landy an advantage, but the doctor from Harrow would have nothing of it and cruised in with ease to qualify for the final. Landy qualified in an equally easy heat, running across the line with two other athletes without exerting himself. The mile final was scheduled for the final day of the Games. The night before the greatest mile race in history Landy, unable to sleep, took a short stroll, during which he cut his foot on a piece of broken glass. He insisted that the doctor who treated him (four stitches were needed) should keep the incident secret. But Bannister had problems too; he was getting a cold that he had picked up, possibly in a local swimming pool. Neither, it seemed, was 100 per cent fit, making it appear to be a battle of the infirm rather than the Titans.

Before the race the zany Australian coach, Percy Cerutty, who had, for a short period, advised Landy, penned two letters to him offering advice on how the race should be run. The basic recommendation was that Landy should take the first lap easy but with three laps to go make his effort, in essence, making it a three-lap race. Landy binned the advice without opening the letters. He had been unhappy with Cerutty's methods and his bizarre attitudes towards his charges. Among other things, Cerutty had woken him while he was trying to get a good night's sleep before his race at the 1952 Olympics. When admonished, Cerutty said athletes did not need much sleep.

It was hot – too hot for a marathon, the event which the road runners had started at 12.30 p.m. and, when the mile was ready to start, were two hours into their inhuman grind. The Englishman and holder of the world's fastest time, Jim Peters, who allegedly trained three times per day, was well in the lead. In the stadium, with the foothills of the snow-capped Rocky Mountains as a backdrop, was a packed crowd of 35,000 spectators. Locals, Europeans and track fans from the US west coast had turned up to see the 'miracle mile', the only two four-minute milers in the world slugging it out to see who was the champion. Bannister, wearing the red rose of England on his vest, and Landy adorned with a map outline of 'God's Own Country', stressed the representational nature of the event – England's Glory v. the man from Down Under, the 'mother country' v. the former colony. By now Landy was the 4:1 favourite but Bannister could not be written off. If anyone else in the final won, it would be the biggest track upset of the century. Few people knew that three times before the race Landy had medical treatment on his cut foot.

The milers got to their marks. The gun went and New Zealander Bill Baillie ran into the lead, followed by the Oxford graduate David Law, running for England. But by 380 yards, rejecting Cerutty's unread advice, Landy took over and strode with his economical style to the end of the first lap in 58.2s. Bannister was five yards down, the rest of the field trailing behind. As suspected, it was going to be a two-man race. Landy would make the pace and Bannister would hope to out-sprint him. Landy did everything he possibly could. Again there was colonial symbolism – the colonial as a beast of burden, providing the Englishman with a free ride in the production of a result. Would a victory for Landy be read as a kind of colonial resistance? Landy himself saw it as a contest between the hunter and the hunted − the responsibility for the race being with the hunted who had to guess what was happening in the minds of those chasing him.

In the second lap Landy opened a large gap of more than ten yards on his white-clad adversary as he reached the half-mile in 1m. 58.2s. What was Bannister thinking? He needed to close the space; if it opened any further he would become detached, losing touch with the race and losing momentum and motivation. He worked hard on the third lap and by the time they reached the bell was only a yard behind. Closing the gap and the sound of the bell brought the crowd to levels of delirium never heard before in a North American mile. Bannister seemed to have Landy where he wanted him but, to the crowd's astonishment, the Aussie surged and the gap remained as they reached the final furlong. Bannister had never run so far without utilising his famous sprint. Had Landy snuffed it out? It seemed so as the gap opened slightly as they approached home.

Then the fans witnessed one of sport's great dramatic moments. Rounding the turn Landy, anxious about Bannister's position, turned his head to glance over his inside shoulder (Figure 5.2). At that very moment Bannister passed him on the outside, opening up a perceptible lead. Landy may have been demoralised but he didn't show it. He continued running at the same pace, not letting the gap widen. The two runners maintained this format as they reached the tape, Bannister crossing the line a yard or so ahead, his face contorted in agony. His time was a personal best − 3m. 58.8s, just over half-a-second faster than at Oxford. He had beaten the world record holder who also recorded his second four-minute mile, 0.8s behind the winner. Bannister was shattered, just like his physical state at the end of the Oxford race. Landy appeared far from spent. Bannister couldn't stand up and while the two athletes apparently embraced each other, some read this body language as Landy supporting the exhausted winner.

About half-an-hour after the 'miracle mile' the crowd witnessed another spectacle, the finish of the marathon. This was to be the

Figure 5.2 Bannister overtakes Landy in the Empire Games mile final,
Vancouver, 1954 (Copyright photo by Charles Warner)

downside of serious running – the agony replacing the ecstasy. The
English marathon runner, Jim Peters, in the lead, had dramatically
collapsed in the stadium, dehydrated and his running reduced to an
uncontrolled stagger. In a ghastly parody of 'sport' he never reached
the finishing line, rescued from further danger by Games officials. He
was immediately placed in an ambulance and hospitalised.

The English team returned home but Roger Bannister remained in
Vancouver. In doing so he was able to demonstrate that the distance

between him and the non-Oxbridge athletes was not quite as wide as some had assumed. Bannister, the recently qualified doctor, offered to stay for a week with Peters and the team manager. He felt he could be of help. Peters was touched by this generous gesture.

ONE FINAL JOB

There was one final job to do before Bannister followed Jim Peters into the world of retired runners and got on with other (more serious) things. A medical career beckoned. Surely, with his heroic status other things would fall into place too. A perfect season would be complete if he could lift the European 1,500 metres title, to be contested in Switzerland later in August. The European championships were a step above the Empire Games in terms of the quality of the competition; they were second only to the Olympics. There would be no obvious pacemaker in this race. Roger Bannister faced what was arguably the hardest race of his life. Inevitably, he carried the burden of favourite.

The fifth European athletics championships were held at a cosy stadium in Bern with world class athletes in almost every event. The competition in the middle-distance races would be intense. Bannister, running the 1,500 metres, might not have an individual opponent of the calibre of Landy but there could be no doubting the depth of talent that would appear in the final. Bannister had experienced his most arduous season. The four-minute mile had been back in May. Three-and-a-half months later he was required to complete an arguably harder task: he had to race to victory without the help of a willing pacemaker.

Bannister found his heat easy and qualification for the final was almost a formality. Bannister's sprinting ability brought him home comfortably. The final was a different matter. It turned out to be a bit of a rough house with one of the runners being knocked over in the early rush. It was a 'scrambling' event, the sort Bannister disliked, and he stayed near the back of the pack, keeping out of harm's way. At 800 metres the race was led by Bannister's conqueror earlier in the season,

Jungwirth of Czechoslovakia. The pace, 2m. 2s, was comfortable enough but with some good fast finishers in the field anything could still happen. In Britain, listening to their wireless sets, some fans wondered if Bannister could do it again. It had been a long season and now the nation was asking him to deliver the final flourish. Jungwirth was turning out to be the pacemaker and was still in the lead at 1,200 metres in 3m. 4.3s with Bannister close behind in a good striking position. The relatively slow pace was playing into Bannister's hands. The Dane, Gunnar Nielsen, at one time tipped as a contender for the first four-minute mile, looked threatening and was well known for his sprint finish. With 300 metres to go Bannister shot off; only Nielsen could follow him, the rest of the field left wallowing. Bannister's speed was close to that he achieved in the AAA championships, but off a much faster pace. Nielsen could not hold on and Bannister broke the tape about five metres clear (Figure 5.3). It all appeared easier than

Figure 5.3 Bannister's last race: winning the European 1,500 metres championship, Bern, 1954. In second place is Gunnar Nielsen of Denmark (Topfoto)

people had expected. His last 200 metres was timed at 25s, his final time was 3m. 43.8s. Bannister, at his peak, could be a winner and a champion in a truly run race. Norris McWhirter dubbed him 'The Compleat Miler'. For his final race, at least, this tired reference to Izaak Walton, seemed justified.

It had been a remarkable season and in a worldwide press poll Roger Bannister became the first Englishman to be voted Sportsman of the Year, closely followed by the distance runner Vladimir Kuts. Third was John Landy. The overall vote was clear but a large number of newspapers placed Landy above Bannister and the great French daily sports paper, *L'Equipe*, didn't include him in their top five. The Soviet sports paper *Sovietsky Sport* didn't even rank Bannister in their top ten. He was not universally applauded – but, after all, this was the Cold War. But even in the UK it was Chataway who won the BBC Sports Personality of the Year award (Bannister gained second place) – something of a surprise to Bannister's fans. It was probably Chataway's nail-biting victory over Vladimir Kuts, televised live late in the season, that remained fresh in the minds of the televiewers who sent in their votes. Was the world's press more or less discerning than the British television audience?.

Near the end of what many still regard as the most momentous year in the history of British athletics Roger Bannister announced that he had retired from running and would, for two years, devote his time to his work as a house surgeon at St Mary's. He hinted that he might return to running at the end of that two year stint, but doubted it – and he never did. He predicted 3m. 55s for the mile 'some day' and thought that the limit of human endurance may not be reached until the time was reduced to 3m. 50s. But by mid-August, 1975, that barrier too had been broken.

For some years after 6 May 1954, Bannister presented a necktie, designed by his wife, to all those who had achieved the four-minute mile. It was a sort of elite club for those who had broken the barrier. Eventually, he had to stop making this award because he was giving too many ties away. The four-minute mile had become passé. The margin of improvement of his record was made to look modest when, in 1957 Herb Elliott ran 3m. 54.4s to break Derek Ibbotson's 3m. 57.2s, the time that broke Landy's record. Bannister's mistake in distributing the ties was that he thought that the four-minute mile would always be seen as a worthy achievement, somewhat paradoxical in view of his prediction in 1994 that a 3m. 30s mile was possible. We will see. At the time of writing the record is held by Hicham El Guerrouj of Morocco with a time of 3m. 43.13s. Schoolboys, and a 40-year-old, have run sub-four-minute miles; about 1,000 athletes have done so and it has been achieved over 5,000 times. The American, Steve Scott, ran it 137 times. Some people are surprised that no woman has yet run under four minutes, the world women's record at the time of writing standing at 4m. 12.56s, run by the Russian, Svetlana Masterkova.

BANNISTER'S BOOK

Roger Bannister's final major engagement with serious running was his self-representation in its history. In 1955 Putnam's Publishers of London produced Roger Bannister's book titled First Four Minutes, the nearest thing that exists to his autobiography. It might be more accurately called a memoir. He claimed to have written it in six weeks though for years he had obviously been taking notes of his races and his training. It was reprinted in the same year. Bannister was still only 26. The first edition carried the comment that half the royalties would be given to the AAA Coaching Fund – an interesting recipient in view of Bannister's dislike of coaching. More recently he stated that half the royalties went towards building a running track at Wealdstone. A Corgi paperback edition of First Four Minutes came out in 1957, price two shillings and six pence, available in high street bookshops and railway station bookstalls (Figure 5.4). Later, as mass running became increasingly popular, two editions were published in the USA, one in 1981 and the other in 1994. Bannister added an 'Introduction' to each. Fifty years after the 'dream mile' another edition was published with a new epilogue.

(a)

(b)

Figure 5.4 Bannister's book. The author's well-thumbed copy (a); one of the American editions (b) (photographs by Alan Bailey)

By the standards of sports (auto)biographies the book achieved pretty good sales. And it is well written, as one would expect from an Oxford man, though like most sports biographies it concentrates mainly on sports with the 'big event' being the focal point of the entire book. It tells us almost nothing about Bannister's private life, nor what he got up to with his chums, except the occasional lark and running with them. There is not the slightest suggestion that the book was 'ghosted'.

Being a scientist and a runner, it is hardly surprising that a good deal of scientific detail is found in the book; Bannister's training methods, aspects of bio-mechanics and physiology, different forms of training, a list of his races and his ideas on coaching. After all, this is what athletics fans wanted. Yet the book has an intensely humanistic touch that, at times, shows the hero as inevitably human. Training the body required hardness but writing the First Four Minutes included a softer touch. For example, during the Empire Games, Bannister renewed his acquaintance with Landy whom he had first met in the Helsinki Olympics two years earlier. While in Vancouver, Bannister, in the company of Chris Chataway, spotted Landy training. He considered passing by on the other side and admitted that he would have been too embarrassed to introduce himself had Chataway not been present too. As the world's two four-minute milers met, Bannister tells us that he 'was conscious of blushing' but Landy showed 'no sense of awkwardness'. And then, having broken the ice, Bannister masterfully described the inevitable homoeroticism of running:

> He [Landy] faced me bare-chested, wearing only running shorts. His dark curly hair was cut short and his tough body bronzed by the sun. He had been running barefoot on the grass between harder bursts on the cinder track. He had a most attractive personality and seemed most friendly.

Later, Bannister added that Landy was 'the sort of runner I could never become, and for this I admire him'.

Bannister's lyrical description of Landy is matched by his frequent romantic allusions in First Four Minutes to different kinds of running from that of the track racer. His descriptions of running in the Welsh and Scottish mountains display a softer, feminine side to his personality, a sensuous engagement with nature rather than the anaesthetic description he gives of his training, full of statistics, tactics and plans. As a schoolboy he recalled the feeling of being weighed down, constrained, by school uniform and books: he wanted to throw away such daily burdens and frolic freely. In his book he regularly returns to the theme of escape. But escape from what? The answer, I think, is the constraints and regimen of daily life, the machine, the city, the running track.

A famous description, reproduced in several other books, describes his childhood desire for freedom through running barefoot on the beach:

> I remember the moment when I stood barefoot in firm dry sand by the sea. The air had a special quality as if it had a life of its own. The sound of breakers on the shore shut out all others. I looked up at the clouds, like great white-sailed galleons, chasing proudly inland. I looked at the regular ripples in the sand, and could not absorb so much beauty. … At this supreme moment I leapt in sheer joy. I was startled, and frightened, by the tremendous excitement that so few steps could create. I glanced around uneasily to see if anyone was watching. A few more steps – self-consciously now and firmly gripping the original excitement. The earth seemed to move with me. I was running now, and a fresh rhythm entered my body. No longer conscious of my movement I discovered a new unity with nature.

Are these the words of a scientist or a poet? Bannister's love of nature, the wildness of landscape and the sensuousness of running reflect a different side to the man whose public life was focused on the accurately measured 440 yards track and the fifth of a second hand of the stopwatch. On the beach there was no track, except the prints in the sand left by his feet. And time failed to matter.

First Four Minutes also contains Bannister's vivid recollections of running in the mountains at times when he simply wanted to distance himself from the geometry of the track, to leave its time and space constraints and revel in the mountains and moors of Wales and Scotland. He recalls, in lyrical and somewhat homoerotic mode, the experience of running following a rock-climbing trip to Snowdonia:

> The wind sang in our ears and deafened us. Sometimes we tumbled, falling if we were lucky on a patch of grass, otherwise on hostile stones. We picked out likely landing places, as we jumped on ledge or boulder. Faster and faster we ran, each in turn leading until he slipped and was overtaken. Towards the bottom we could release ourselves from the agony of checking our descent, that tore at the overworked muscles of our thighs. It was a glorious moment when the level ground brought us under control.
>
> At Penn-y-Pass [sic] we threw ourselves on the grass by the stream, and drank our fill of water. Then we rolled over on our backs and lay there, steamy perspiration rising from clothes that had been inadequate protection against the chill wind on the ridges. We had drunk too deeply of the dangerous mountain air, become too infatuated with the goddess of speed. Waiting to catch up with ourselves we rubbed our aching limbs, tired but happy.

Bannister also recalls, again in emotional mode, the recuperative effects of a wild landscape, this time in Kintyre in Scotland following a hard racing season in 1951:

> I felt I was running back to all the primitive joy that my season had destroyed. ... The gulls were crying overhead and a herd of wild goats were silhouetted against the headland. I started to run again with the sun in my eyes nearly blinding me. I could barely distinguish slippery rock from heathery turf or bog; yet my feet did not slip or grow weary now – they had new life and confidence. I ran in a frenzy of speed, drawn by an unseen force. The sun sank, setting the forest ablaze, and turning the sky to dull smoke. Then tiredness came on and my bleeding feet tripped me. I rolled down a heather-topped bank and lay there happily exhausted.

The playful gambolling in Snowdonia was followed immediately by a time-trial on the quarter-mile cinder circuit where, a year before the four-minute mile, he ran three-quarters of a mile, unpaced in 3m. 1s. And the Scottish adventure was soon followed by a personal best performance over 1,500 metres, even though, with the usual Oxford understatement, Bannister claimed to be 'completely out of training'.

The poetic references to his love and the lure of the wild signify that Bannister distinguished very clearly between running and racing. Running, represented by Landy's unclothed upper body and the wildness of nature, had a purity that was missing in racing with its carefully cultured quarter-mile track and the protocols of competition. Bannister wrote that the 'athlete is essentially a *wild animal* who has brought himself under control except for the *primitive passion* unleashed in his athletic efforts' (italics added). Even so, such passion, unleashed too early or too late, could (as in other contexts) result in failure. Reversions to the primitive had to be managed and controlled.

Although in *First Four Minutes* he displayed distaste for intellectualising about running, he admitted to be fascinated with the philosophical question of why athletes run. Indeed, the subject 'had tended to over-shadow [his] interest in [his] own running'. He appeared to favour disport, *jouissance* and the visceral pleasures it provided over sport in its modern guise, with its constraints of time and space. It was hardly surprising, therefore, that having retired from racing after the European championships he continued running for purposes of good health, rather than victories and records – what would later be termed 'fun running' or jogging. And occasionally he took part in orienteering – the most ecological kind of running where attention is paid to details in the landscape, not to the finishing line.

LIFE AFTER RACING

Bannister's book marked the end of his running career. Indeed, he would have been labelled a professional and thence banned from amateur competition if he had continued serious running and racing following the book's publication. He had, however, written and published academic papers as that was considered part of his job. But the highlight of his career, as viewed by the mass public, was never going to be his medical work.

Bannister's life moved on. He proceeded to earn and obtain a large number of degrees (many honorary) and a list of other credentials as long as your arm. These included a CBE ('Commander of the British Empire') in 1955 and, in the same year, the status of married man. He wed Moyra Jacobsson, the daughter of former Swedish banker, Per Jacobsson who held the lofty position of Chairman and Managing Director of the International Monetary Fund from 1956 to 1963. National Service eventually caught up with Bannister when, in 1957, he was at last called up – as a lieutenant in the Royal Army Medical Corps. Many more honours were to follow, including the knighthood, awarded for his 'services to sport'.

Between 1963 and 1985 Bannister published or contributed to a large number of academic papers. If his more popular writing is included it seems reasonable to say that he authored (or mainly co-authored) well over 100 papers – a solid academic output. In the early part of his academic career Bannister's oeuvre combined his interests in running with that of medicine. In 1954, for example, he published a paper in the Practitioner entitled 'Stress and sport'; in 1956 one on 'Muscular effort' in the British Medical Bulletin; in 1967 'Medical aspects of competitive athletics' in the Transactions of the Medical Society of London, and in 1972, 'Sport, physical recreation and the national health' in the British Medical Journal. All this was going on while he penned papers for more popular publications, including a chapter on 'The psychological approach' in a book about the experiences of top-class athletes, authored entirely by members of the Achilles Club. Trained in physiology and neurology, it is not clear how qualified Bannister was to write on psychology but the article was not without interest. As time went on his writing and research moved away from the legacy of running and focused much more on neurology. Writing on the Olympics and on training for the young athlete was a considerable distance away from

'Laryngeal electromyography in multiple system atrophy with autonomic failure', and a fair amount of his time as a neurologist seems to have been taken up editing Lord Brain's standard textbook on *Clinical Neurology*, first published in 1960. From the third edition onward it was revised by Sir Roger and soon became known as *Brain and Bannister's Clinical Neurology*. He also edited a hefty tome on *Autonomic Failure*. Medical scientists are not into writing books as much as their social science cousins and in terms of book production he was more known as an editor than an author. His only written (as opposed to edited) book cited in his c.v. (in *Who's Who?*) is *First Four Minutes*.

Despite an apparently conventional career he could, as I will show, continue, from time to time, to arouse controversy. However, he could never shake off the tag of 'the four-minute miler', despite the fact that the world mile record moved progressively further and further away from four minutes.

SOME MORE CONTROVERSIES

The publication of his memoir was not quite the end of Bannister's engagement with running though he cannot be said to have made any further significant contribution to it. From time to time he talked and wrote about it, and his work with the Sports Council kept him in touch with the broader arena of sports. He continued to be a global traveller, attending conferences and sitting on committees almost all over the world. Many of these also reignited an engagement with sports.

There were, however, several somewhat controversial athletics-related incidents that brought Bannister back into the headlines. The first occurred in 1957 when the *New York Times* carried a front-page story related to the dramatic growth – Bannister had predicted a 'deluge' – in the number of four-minute miles since Hägg's record was first broken. By 1957 what was formerly a 'barrier' had been broken 18 times by 12 athletes. This could be explained in at least three ways. First, there had been a growth in the number of young men taking up running in the post-war period. Second, having been demonstrated that a four-minute mile was possible, it was no longer a 'psychological' barrier (if it ever had been – see Chapter 6). The third, and most sensational, explanation was the one offered in the *New York Times* article. In it, Dr Herbert Berger, a drug addiction expert and a consultant to the US Public Health Service, averred that it was amphetamine, sold under the name Benzedrine, which had made it possible for more athletes to achieve sub-four-minute times. I have already referred to Gordon Pirie's statement about the widespread use of stimulants in the world of foot-racing and in medical and other magazines frequent use was made of images of athletes to advertise the sale of stimulants and other drugs. But Berger's views took amphetamine out of the sports books and medical magazines on to the front page of a major national daily.

No names were mentioned but the 12 runners who had broken four minutes were implicated. The most famous was, of course, Roger Bannister who robustly denied any knowledge of drug use. As noted earlier, in *First Four Minutes* he obliquely alluded to artificial aids to running in his comments on practical ways of breathing high concentrations of oxygen. The use of oxygen had been associated with Australian swimmers and mountaineers climbing Mount Everest. Bannister was quoted as saying that 'all records would be beaten were we to administer oxygen to athletes in a manner similar to the one used in connection with the victorious team of Everest climbers'. His personal view seemed to be that such help was not ethically justifiable and that such assistance was not permissible for the four-minute mile. Some medicos felt such assistance would be tantamount to 'doping' while others felt that any benefit of inhaling oxygen before a race would only have resulted from suggestion. This has not prevented Tim Noakes, the runner-scientist-author of the 1,000-page tome, *Lore of Running*, from recently speculating that it 'is perhaps possible that Sir Roger ran the four-minute mile because of the experimental runs he performed in the research laboratory at Oxford while inhaling oxygen-enriched air'.

In connection with the suggestion that the increase in the number of four-minute miles had been induced by the use of stimulants, Bannister did 'not believe the charge', adding that he knew of no runners who had ever used stimulants. This could be read as a surprising comment, given his role as a medical scientist and international athlete. It certainly contradicted Pirie's comments about the widespread use of Benzedrine, and reflected a rather cloistered view. However, Bannister's statement was supported by Sir Adolphe Abrahams, by then the Honorary Medical Officer of the British Olympic team, who added that the four-minute mile 'owes nothing to amphetamine (or any other drugs)'. This is not to deny, however, that Sir Adolphe was fully aware of the problem of deciding when drug use in sport could be justified and when it should be banned. Drug use, he felt, was not inevitably 'unsporting'. Indeed, it could be argued that it is exactly what one would expect given the pressures to succeed in modern achievement-oriented sport.

As time went on, the debates about performance-enhancement went off into various other directions and became focused much more on the allegations and subsequent proof of steroid abuse on both sides of the former 'Iron Curtain'. The link between the improvement of the mile record and the taking of 'banned' substances was rarely made. This was especially the case when the athletes were assumed to be 'clean' because they were British (Steve Ovett, Sebastian Coe, Steve Cram) or, later, because spurious 'racial' factors could be used to 'explain' the success of the world mile record holders because they were 'Africans' (for example, Filbert Bayi, Kipchoge Keino or Hicham El Geurrouj). However, Bannister's coach, adviser and/or friend, Stampfl, later went to work in Australia where he was regarded, as noted earlier, as a 'hard man'. According to at least one observer, Werner Reiterer in his book *Positive!*, Stampfl was not unaware of the possible benefits of anabolic steroids.

Bannister appears to have been conservative in his pronouncements on sport, sometimes to the point of naivety. In 1979, in one of his articles written for *Sports Illustrated*, he made several observations that would have made progressives choke on his words. He first suggested, in a discussion on sport and politics, that those who wanted to boycott the Nazi Olympics of 1936 were wrong, adding that the four gold medals won by Jesse Owens had put 'paid to Hitler's view of Aryan supremacy'. If, by this, he meant that issues of 'race' in sport disappeared following Owens's exploits, he seems wide of the mark. Here was surely a massive inflation of the importance of running and as subsequent events showed, Bannister's words hardly reflected the historical case. Once the temporarily sanitised Games were over Hitler reverted to his rabid racism about the superiority of the 'Nordic race'. Indeed, at the same time Hitler seems to have argued that, as a result of what he read as their animal-like qualities, it was black athletes, not 'Aryans', who were naturally supreme. In future Games, he stated, black athletes would be banned because of their perceived unfair advantage. And racist rhetoric concerning black athletes is hardly dead and buried today.

Additionally, Bannister was virtually hoist by his own petard when he stated in the same article that the world long jump record, achieved in Mexico City by Bob Beamon, should, 'in fairness', be labelled as 'altitude assisted'. Sir Roger seemed to have forgotten his own world record and the human assistance that he had capitalised on at the time, an observation pointed out in a letter to the editor in a subsequent edition.

A more controversial incident, that made the national press in Bannister's post-athletic years, occurred in 1996 by which time track racing had moved on from the halcyon days of the 1950s. Steroids had replaced amphetamines, Africans had succeeded Europeans, and the world mile record stood at 3m. 44.39s. Attitudes and knowledge about the sport had changed. And Bannister again became entangled in a subject barely commented upon in British athletics circles in the early 1950s: that of sport and 'race'.

At the 1996 meeting of the British Association for the Advancement of Science, Sir Roger, then aged 67, thought it worth discussing what he felt were the 'natural advantages' that blacks had in running. At the time this was, and remains, a highly controversial subject. He said that it was 'perfectly obvious' (that is, 'common sense') that there must be something special about their anatomy or physiology that produced their success. It seems that he had, unwittingly thrown himself into a maelstrom of debate, controversy, and, as he admitted, the arena of political incorrectness. It is possible that his reactions may have been influenced by a 1950s mind-set also held by his old Oxford friend, Norris McWhirter. In the early 1960s McWhirter felt confident enough to classify the best-ever athletic performances by what he termed 'White' and 'Negro' athletes. He also used terms such as 'the negro *race*' (italics added) and supported theories of bone and skeletal differences. Looking at his two columns of data, headed bizarrely 'Caucasiforms' and 'Negriforms', his readers could draw what conclusions they wanted to about the respective ability of the two 'races' in different events. For example, it was shown to be 'obvious' that 'black' runners were inferior to 'whites' in the middle and long distance events.

Bannister's statements elicited a considerable backlash in both the popular press and in academic debate. The British sociologist, Brett St Louis, writing in *Body and Society*, has recalled Bannister's 'self-consciously ignorant curiosity over long-defunct racial notions of skeletal differences and climatic adaptation'. The American scholar John Hoberman suggested that Bannister exemplified the 'scientific imprecision' that had typified the history of racial thinking. Bannister was seen to be uninformed about 'ideas he appeared to be tossing off the top of his head'. He had cited proposals about the 'racial' differences in the length of the Achilles tendon that had seldom been mentioned since the 1930s; he claimed that he could separate the scientific from the sociological (all sciences are *social* sciences); and in the end he admitted that he didn't really know the true reasons for so-called 'racial' variations in athletic performance. Hoberman summarised Bannister's presentation as 'a strikingly *amateurish* performance by a professional scientist' (italics added). Here, less opaquely than anywhere else, is seen a shadow of the racialist ideology implicit in the writings of his friends, Norris and Ross McWhirter. In a rather sad end to his, by now, very occasional engagement with serious running, Roger Bannister was seen to be exposing himself as a true amateur.

6

FINISHING LINES

The writing of Sir Roger Bannister as runner did not end with the publication of his book. Authors – academic and popular (if that's not a false distinction) – have continued to write about him. Much of this writing reflects a particularly English nostalgia, a quest for something past in the ever-changing present. Bannister has been eulogised as the gentleman amateur, one of my points of departure at the start of this book. But as shown in the previous chapter a parallel flow of writing has been more critical, adding to the negative comments that, from time to time, accompanied his running career and thereafter. A focus on how Bannister, the runner, has been written about since 1960 leads me to a concluding evaluation of Roger Bannister.

CRITICAL VOICES

In 1961 a revisionist version of Bannister's running career was penned by one his contemporaries, Gordon Pirie. The runners' runner and a fanatical trainer, Pirie had always felt ambivalent about Bannister ('As a person I found him unpredictable', he wrote) and dubbed his running career 'a fleeting appearance on the scene'. In Pirie's autobiography, *Running Wild*, he displayed respect for Bannister's running but presented a critical insight, reflecting the views of many athletes and fans in the 1950s. Pirie made five critical points:

1   Bannister trained specifically for a single event and made the mistake of not training hard throughout the year;
2   most of his best performances were paced;
3   he saved himself for big events and picked his races carefully;
4   he obtained privileges from the governing bodies that were denied other runners, i.e. travelling abroad unaccompanied by officials;
5   he misled young runners by giving the impression that he trained lightly.

Pirie also argued that Bannister could have run much faster with more training, based more on the methods of Gerschler and Reindel. He suggested, for example, that with maximum training Bannister could have run 3m. 50s in 1954.

Also in 1961, Bannister was denigrated in the US publication, *Track Newsletter*. A somewhat spurious quantitative study sought to rank the greatest milers of all time. No more than seven years after the Oxford event, the authors ranked Bannister only eighth. They justified his relatively lowly placing on the grounds that 'in five seasons of competition he ran less than 20 races at the mile distance', that the 'clinical exactness' that typified his planning meant that 'his running lacked any spontaneity', that his 'races were few and far between' and that 'he rarely met the top men of his time': scathing perhaps, but not totally inaccurate.

Criticism of Bannister also came from Percy Cerutty. In 1952, at a pre-Olympic meet in London, he had approached the English runner and said: 'So, *you're* Bannister ... We've come to *do* you'. Following Bannister's retirement he was equally forthright about the four-minute miler's career. In his 1964 book, *Middle Distance Running*, Cerutty observed that Bannister 'failed to achieve the pinnacle of greatness by adding more world records, or in winning Olympic gold medals'. Cerutty's runners, *contra* Bannister, were urged to race, not run; they must always try to adopt 'the tradesman's attitude and be able to perform at super-normal levels every time' they raced. Bannister's small number of races was seen as 'a very immature approach'. Throughout the 1960s criticisms of Bannister's methods of 'racing' kept resurfacing. The Australian runner, Ron Clarke, saw the four-minute mile as having been achieved in 'artificial circumstances', meaning 'careful attention to pre-arranged pacemaking'.

More recently, some British sports writers have matched these critical modes of representing Roger Bannister. In 2001, a vote was taken among journalists to determine the 'Supreme British Sporting Performance of the past 100 Years'. What won? Well, Bannister's four-minute mile. The athletics correspondent of *The Guardian*, John Rodda, stated that Bannister had been 'ludicrously placed' first and that he 'couldn't hold a candle' to those British runners who, on the one hand had won Olympic gold medals, and on the other, possessed more durable world records. 'The mile was not even an Olympic event' stated another journalist and, with a *coup de grâce*, added yet another voice criticising his methods: 'in cold reality [Bannister] was paced in a highly contrived race'.

An indication that Bannister made a limited impact on the British cultural imagination is shown by the results of a BBC telephone poll in 2002 to establish who viewers and listeners thought were the top 100 Britons of all time. The results showed that there was no place for Roger Bannister (but none either for Prince Charles and Laurence Olivier). 'All time' is a long time but in the minds of the poll's respondents, in the second millennium Roger Bannister emerges as a less significant figure than Boy George and Johnny Rotten, David Beckham and Donald Campbell. He is not the much loved hero that some suggest.

However, these critiques miss the point of Bannister's running. As I have shown, there was a streak in him that hated racing; hence his seeming preference for paced events on the one hand, and for frolicking in the mountains on the other. His true love was for a more child-like running where freedom and frolic rather than discipline and constraint were paramount. Bannister stopped racing and became wealthy; Pirie carried on running and breaking records but died poor. For Bannister, enough was enough. For Pirie enough was never enough. Bannister reflected a view of sustainability, Pirie one of over-specialisation – an addiction to racing that was ultimately unsustainable. Put in the terms of sports scholar Jeffrey Segrave, Pirie entered the world of serious sport to live; Bannister did so to visit.

Academic writers seem to have been kinder to Bannister, reflecting a kind of nostalgic, class-based British sports history. For example, the doyen of British sports historians, Richard Holt, has suggested that the four-minute mile was a last flourish of amateur heroics and an example of chivalry (a view also held by Franz Stampfl) in which 'two first-class athletes [Chataway and Brasher] sacrificed themselves to permit Bannister to break a record' – seemingly written as a chivalric triangle. But as I have observed earlier, there was no sacrifice. Only Bannister could have won that race; the other two aided him, were his acolytes, assistants, part of his team. And it is not much of a sacrifice when you ran a personal best time, as Chataway did. Indeed, in the May 1954 issue of *Athletics World*, which professional historians seemingly missed, the McWhirter twins were keen to point out that it was a 'miserable misconception' to talk of the 'self sacrifice of the two Christophers', stressing instead team spirit but also mentioning Bannister's ambition.

More recently, Richard Holt and Tony Mason, in their book, *Sport in Britain 1945–2000*, again described the four-minute mile as proof that in the 1950s 'the true amateur could still excel' in the world of record breaking. It was 'a triumph for the amateur spirit of British athletics, a team effort with a touch of undergraduate innocence'. The use of the adjective 'undergraduate' is, presumably, an attempt to nostalgically romanticise the event since, at the time of the race, neither Bannister, Chataway nor Brasher were undergraduates. The race was a sophisticated, coldly calculated and planned record attempt rather than some sort of college romp. There was nothing innocent about it. Holt and Mason's romantic description of a bygone age may have been an ironic reflection of the views of the old buffers who ran British athletics at the time. My reading of it is that it is nothing less than a *misreading* of sports history.

Consider also Garry Whannel's distinction between sportsmanship and victory. 'In the last 30 years', he writes, 'following Roger Bannister's four-minute mile, the ethos of the English sporting gentleman has been challenged by the new individualistic drive for success'. This, I think, is an exaggeration and I sense that individualism was a feature of most of the runners described in the previous pages, including Bannister. None of them was more individualistic than Nurmi. Wooderson too was surely a one-off, Jack Lovelock even more so – highly idiosyncratic, a loner and obsessed with the 'perfect race'. Bannister was also clearly an individualist, self-described as a 'misfit', accused for doing his own thing. In all of these runners the 'drive for success' was phenomenal. And, while Bannister may have possessed the image of the sportsman he displayed a preference for employing pacemakers – human machines – in most of his big 'races'. This was not, technically speaking, bad sportsmanship (i.e. cheating) but it had certainly laid him open to accusations of failing to undertake a well-run race. To suggest, as Arthur Daley of the *New York Times* did, that in the 6 May spectacle 'the competition was ideal' only made any sense if he meant that there was no competition.

Even though the Vancouver 'mile of the century' was technically a championship competition and a real race, it turned out to be a paced event with only two men really in it. Landy would always be the pacemaker in such a contest. His front running permitted Bannister to win and to set a personal best. In his competitions Bannister wanted to be first in the most optimal way possible, that is, to have been paced by a colleague, as part of a plan (as with Chataway) or as part of a race (as by Landy). Recall some of Bannister's best results (see Table 6.1). The significance of pacemaking in his key performances is clear.

As I noted earlier, for the likes of Montague Shearman, writing in the 1880s, these paced performances would not have been seen as

Table 6.1 Bannister's best results

Year	Distance	Time	Result
1951	¾ mile	2m. 56.8s	1st – paced (second fastest ever)
1952	¾ mile	2m. 52s	paced time trial (world's fastest ever)
1952	1,500 m.	3m. 46s	4th – raced (Olympic final, British record)
1953	one mile	4m. 3.6s	1st – paced (British record)
1953	one mile	4m. 2s	1st – paced (fastest ever British result, but not ratified as a record)
1954	one mile	3m. 59.4s	1st – paced (world record)
1954	one mile	3m. 58.8s	1st – raced/paced (Empire Games, British record)
1954	1,500 m.	3m. 43.8s	1st – raced (European championships, British record)

truly-run races. He would certainly not have thought those involved in such practices to be good sportsmen. This prejudice (if prejudice it be) against paced record attempts was still around during the 1950s. Derek Ibbotson commented that 'it would have a bad effect on running if such manufactured records became more important than winning a good race'. Although Bannister proved able to win good races, he admitted, 'I always found it easier if I did not have to lead all the way'. This is, of course, a totally rational approach.

'GENTLEMAN AMATEUR'?

The last couple of chapters have surely destroyed any notion that Bannister was an 'amateur' in the 'gentleman amateur' sense of the term, yet in 1999 British sports sociologists were still able to describe him as an athlete in the 'the noble amateur tradition'. Applied to world-class British runners of the 1950s, including the Oxford group, it was impossible to take an 'amateur' approach to the sport and remain 'world-class'. However, the term 'amateur' is slippery so I think it is worth returning to the 'gentleman amateur' tag that has become attached to Bannister and which has been my main bone of contention throughout this book.

Regarding the adjective 'gentleman', Bannister may have been a gentle man but adding the word 'amateur' changes the meaning somewhat and Lincoln Allison, in his book *Amateurism in Sport*, devotes nine pages to an appendix on 'The concept of the amateur and amateurism', citing numerous definitions and applications. Well, Bannister as an athlete was certainly not 'amateurish' in the derogatory sense of being a dabbler. On the other hand, in the literal sense of the word, that is, a *love* of running, Bannister *was* an amateur. Of that I have no doubt. He admitted that the prime reason for running was to enjoy it, rather than doing people good. He embraced a sensuous, rather than a welfare, justification for running. He chose running, in part, to enrich experience but social forces helped shape his choice. He could *produce* records and victories but also *consume* running. Moreover, he could treat it as social and cultural *capital*.

His own view, as presented in *First Four Minutes*, was that the 'true amateur' was one who fitted 'running into the rest of life until one's work becomes too demanding'. If this was the case, however, serious running would continue to be the preserve of an elite group who had the time and space for training. Those whose work was *always* demanding would simply be excluded. Bannister's view, therefore, harks back to a nineteenth-century view that the only amateurs were those who could afford the time to train and reflects his general conservatism. But at least, he explained what he meant. In 1929 the Abrahams brothers were so confused by the archaic amateur rules that 'what constitutes the true amateur [they were] at a loss to define'.

Bannister loved running but he also hated it. So it was not a case of either/or – the reduction of the complexity of a human life to a simple dualism. Really, it depends on what sort of running we are talking about. He wrote that in each season he had put so much effort into training that 'the moment came when I almost hated athletics'. What he came close to hating was racing and the systematic nature of training. The tedium of it became so great that he took himself off to the wildscapes of Scotland or Wales to rediscover the 'primitive joy' of simply running. Running at top level had amounted to what he termed 'a frightening business', given the expectations of record-hungry fans. Amid the mountains and streams he did not have to put up with the deferred gratification – the masochism – of racing and training. The tension between the nature of running and the culture of racing had been there from his earliest days in athletics, though he did not represent it in these terms. The amateur (fun from running) and the 'professional' (hard work for serious racing) co-existed uneasily throughout his career.

Roger Bannister was also an amateur in the bureaucratic sense that, as far as I know, he was not paid money to run though it would be surprising if he wasn't tempted by the many offers that would have existed during the 1950s. But a different interpretation can be made if an amateur is also defined as one who has not sought or received payment or other material rewards from taking part in sport. Bannister certainly benefited materially from having run the four-minute mile. In a devastating critique of the amateur rules in the 1920s, Adolphe and Harold Abrahams noted that an athlete may not have accepted any money from running but he could hardly avoid the kudos gained from publicity and reputation. And, as William J. Goode put it, in his book *The Celebration of Heroes*, prestige (which Bannister undoubtedly possessed) is a *means* to an individual's goals: 'If we command higher prestige than others, we enjoy entrée into socially more desirable circles', people are more pleased to know such heroes who, in turn, are more likely than others to offer opinions on this, that and the other. Would Bannister have been invited to talk on the BBC Home Service (and published in *The Listener*) in December 1954 about world problems such as the Iron Curtain, Christianity and the Soviet Union, had he not been a famous runner with an Oxford pedigree? His prestige opened many doors for him, during and as a result of his running career. After he had retired, he wrote a successful book; he was, for a short time, a BBC sports commentator (a job he performed rather poorly and from which he was quickly dropped), and for a somewhat longer period (1955–62) did a fair amount of sports journalism with the *Sunday Times* and later

Sports Illustrated. Another way of looking at it, his running provided a huge amount of what economists call 'psychic income' – benefits that might be immeasurable but benefits nevertheless. Running success led to growing confidence, foreign travels and cultural capital. A boy who had been bullied at school became, for a while, a global figure, his name known to a constituency way beyond athletics fandom.

However, far from being a kind of throwback to a pre-modern mythical age of amateurism and fair play, Bannister emerges as a thoroughly modern athlete who followed the broad trajectory started by Kolehmainen and Nurmi. Indeed, Nurmi's dictum of planning, persistence and pacing also applied to Bannister (though the two men were in most other respects as different as chalk from cheese). Bannister sought records based on the stopwatch, he trained hard and with scientific principles in mind, he planned his running 'experiments' meticulously, he was dedicated to being the best. This hardly sounds like the 'gentleman amateur' and all that the term connotes.

WHAT SORT OF HERO? WHAT SORT OF MILE?

How about Bannister's heroic status? For some people he still remains a hero. At least, he is included among those recorded in *The Book of British Sporting Heroes*, a lavish volume published by the National Portrait Gallery. But the word 'hero' is as slippery as 'amateur'. Its meaning floats around according to who uses it. I have already shown that among British athletics fandom, Bannister's reputation was highly fractured. And among sports scholars who ruminate about things like sports heroism there is little agreement on what a sports hero is. Indeed some think that the term 'sports hero' is an oxymoron. How could anyone who succeeds in such a banal business as sport achieve the appellation of a hero? Through the four-minute mile Bannister made a sort of mark on sport but he didn't make any difference to sport as an institution, as a form of body-cultural practice. He did not transform society.

Some students of sport feel that you have to be dead to be a hero while others believe that the very notion of the hero in sport perpetuates a kind of infantilism and 'emotional regression'. The trouble with heroes is that the word implies simplicity. As I have tried to show, Roger Bannister was more complicated than he might have first appeared (as, of course, we all are).

Whatever the academics think, among athletics fans the durability of a record is one criterion of heroic status. A man who had held a world mile record for only 46 days would not have been remembered for so long as one who had run the first four-minute mile. The magic of the mile was inextricably connected to the so-called four-minute *barrier*. It was something that could seemingly not be broken. It was an arbitrary time for an arbitrary distance but one that held much significance for the British and North American sporting psyche. Bannister recently claimed, however, that he could never see the psychological side of the four-minute mile. Four minutes is simply a number. It is invested with more importance than it deserves. Those who applaud its significance reflect, I think, a society that, in Oscar Wilde's words, 'knows the price of everything but the value of nothing'.

In the 1950s some British fans (I was one of them) admired runners like Landy or Pirie, or the Soviet, Vladimir Kuts, running from the front and winning, but felt rather less attachment and sympathy for the 'waiter' who hung around in the pack, sprinting past the leader in the closing seconds. There would have been a fair number of middle- and working-class fans and runners who always held Pirie, a non-university runner, as a hero, ahead of Bannister. Many spectators admire dedication, perhaps more than if runners were only there to break records. And while Bannister was very serious about records for several years, he could not be said to have been dedicated to running, or more precisely, racing: medicine, yes, but not foot-racing. This, I think, is greatly to his credit.

The mile was only one of a number of track events for which the period 1945–55 was 'barren' in terms of records. But in other events (e.g. 400, 800, 1,000, 1,500, 5,000 metres) the similar lags that appeared between records cannot be explained by such a 'barrier' as in the case of the conveniently round figures of four minutes (see Table 6.2). In other words, as John Landy has recently pointed out, it was not a psychological barrier that prevented someone running the mile in less than four minutes. Rather, wartime interference with training and international competition, the need in the immediate post-war period for the build up in training appropriate for record-breaking running, and the improved training methods used by athletes by the mid-1950s are more plausible explanations than the notion of a psychological 'barrier'.

Time cannot be stopped at four minutes. The four-minute mile was an invented barrier, fuelled by press hype and by public desire, emerging in a vaguely traceable manner, as invented traditions do. Indeed, the mile has, to an extent, assumed the character of a 'social memory', or a tradition, being rewritten and represented on film and in laudatory books. And the mile is the only imperial measure that continues to have a recognised, official (IAAF ratified) record. The 'tradition' of the mile permits it to be privileged over other imperial distances.

Reminiscing almost 50 years after 1954 Chris Chataway admitted that his generation of British runners were not really all that good – 'only fairly good seems to be the honest answer', he observed in the magazine *Prospect*. His generation ran in the shadow of the Swedes. None of the Britons 'came near to matching Hägg as an athletic phenomenon'. Old Oxford modesty or not, such observations have been rarely articu-

Table 6.2 The barren years of world records. Dates on which world records were set and broken, 1939–55

Event	Date set	Date broken
400 m.	12 August 1939	2 July 1948
800 m.	15 July 1939	3 August 1955
1,500 m.	7 July 1944	4 June 1954
mile	17 July 1945	6 May 1954
5,000 m.	20 September 1942	30 May 1954
10,000 m.	25 August 1944	11 June 1949

lated in the English-bound histories of sport which seem to 'thin out' sports history, focusing only on selected events and ignoring others.

Do today's runners see anything significant in the four-minute mile, the old imperial measure? The distance is rarely run in comparison with the 1,500 metres. It is the 1,500 metres that attracts prize money and esteem. The Commonwealth 1,500 metres champion, Michael East, may represent the post-imperial runner when he says, in Jim Denison's book *Bannister and Beyond*, that 'the future's in the 1,500, and I need to concentrate on that'. It is the 1,500 metres record that he, and other such runners, dream of breaking; it 'carries so much more currency than the mile'. A fast 1,500 gets runners into better races, secures them better funding and improves their chances of getting a sponsor. Runners of East's generation see the mile as something of an irrelevance these days.

Even so, four-minute miles are collected, ranked and listed, just as other collectors save stamps and butterflies. There is a website devoted solely to the four-minute mile. Bannister's memorable event is retained in the public memory by such activities but more so in a much-reproduced photograph of him crossing the line at the finish of the record run (see Figure 5.4). Indeed, it is the photograph of Bannister crossing the line, dressed in angelic white in contrast to the drab ordinariness of the background, head thrown back but maintaining a splendid stride, a climactic moment, that is arguably among the most potent of modern artefacts in the British sporting memory. However, the three hours eight minutes movie, *The Four Minute Mile*, made in 1988 did little to enhance the event in the nation's memory, failing to evoke the nostalgia of the kind generated by *Chariots of Fire*. The three adversaries were painted as shadows of their real selves and the film failed to emotionally involve the viewers.

But have more durable reminders been erected to memorialise, or to concretise, that evening in May 1954, when the nation was said to rejoice in Bannister's battle victory? Not really. In Harrow, the place of his birth, there is a rather nondescript 'Bannister Sports Centre' named

Figure 6.1 Front page news. A memorial to the four-minute mile in the Oxford University Sports Centre (author's photograph)

after him. In Oxford, his athletics memorabilia form a permanent loan to Pembroke College, museumised in a large glass case in the college library but not readily accessed. Calling at the porter's lodge one is told to write to the bursar for permission. On a wall in the university's sports centre, a hugely enlarged copy of the front page of *The Daily Mail* of 7 May 1954 records the event (Figure 6.1). Set in the concrete of the grandstand at Iffley Road is a modest commemorative plaque. Nearby, it has been deemed appropriate to name a cul-de-sac after him – Bannister Close – and there is a small hand-painted board above a

Figure 6.2 Modest monuments to Roger Bannister, Oxford (author's photographs)

gate leading into the university's sports complex that records this place as the site of the first sub-four-minute mile (Figure 6.2). In passing, John Landy – the man who lost the 'miracle mile' – is memorialised to Australians in the same low-key iconography. At Geelong, where he attended school, a modest sign on the fencing enclosing the local running track alludes to Landy's association with it.

When Landy ran in Turku there was a statue of Nurmi in the busy street outside the stadium. Statues of great sporting heroes are not unusual ways in which memories – or records – are sustained. Statues of Stanley Mathews in Stoke-on-Trent, Gareth Edwards in Cardiff and Grete Waitz in Oslo (a veritable city of sporting statues) are examples. The only statue of Bannister and Landy, represented together at the final turn of the 1954 Empire Games mile, is found in Vancouver, Canada. It was cast in bronze by Jack Harman and erected outside the Empire Stadium in 1967. The memorial may represent Canada's success in hosting the Vancouver Games – melding members of the Commonwealth through the shared culture of sport. The two athletes can also be read as representing a joint struggle, human effort and competition. To the non-fan they connote an equality of effort and achievement. They do not represent a *national* victory or hero.

The absence of a statue of Roger Bannister in England, when there is one of Stanley Matthews, suggests, again, that Bannister has not, for any length of time, if ever, been the hero of the masses. Athletics has never matched soccer as the 'people's sport'. Instead, in early 2004, the Royal Mint advertised the sale of 50 pence memorial coins (retailed at £4.95) that celebrated the fiftieth anniversary of Sir Roger's world record. On one side was the Queen's head; on the other Bannister's legs. At about the same time plans were prepared to erect a large plaque in Iffley Road to commemorate Bannister's day of days. Additionally, he claims a place in the National Portrait Gallery, founded in 1856 'to collect the likenesses of famous British men and women'. His representation is by John Ward, drawn in chalk in 1987. He appears as a wise academic, straight-backed, gowned and with book on desk. But surely the reason for him being there is because of his brief running career as much as his work in medicine. Such signs (photos, street names, and portraits), modest though they may be, 'save history'. Public awareness of the four-minute mile is sharpened by the presence of such reminders, encouraging us to compare one sporting site and athletic performance with another. Even the most insignificant sign of commemoration has an effect on the way in which sports history is experienced.

Bannister broke Hägg's mile record but he 'only' (unofficially – on the lone stopwatch held by Ross McWhirter) equalled his 1,500 metres record (admittedly shared with Strand and Lueg). Hägg's 1,500 metres record stood longer than his mile record. Even so, the 'magic' of the mile meant that the breaker of Hägg's 1,500 metres mark, the luckless Santee, was consigned to oblivion. Bettering a time of 3m. 43s seems to have meant little to even the metric world, compared with the 'dream mile' of four minutes. Not for Santee, a picture on the front page of the *Mail*.

A VERY BRIEF VIRTUAL HISTORY

What if the Second World War had not drastically reduced the amount of international sports competition? What if the great Swedish runners of the 1940s, Andersson and Hägg, had not been banned? The doyen of athletics historians, Roberto Quercetani, suggests that it 'is quite possible that another season of joint efforts on the track would have brought either or both under the magic four-minute mile'. Here, Quercetani is unwittingly beginning to indulge in what has become known as counterfactual history; in other words, 'What if…?'. Let me take this 'virtual history' a step further.

Recall that in Malmö, on 15 July 1946, Lennart Strand, full of running, equalled the world 1,500 metres record. What if a mile race, rather than one over only 1,500 metres, had been organised for him? As the mile was frequently run in Sweden, often with the explicit intention of seeking a world record, this is a perfectly plausible possibility. Recall Hägg's comment that, for him also, the four-minute mile was no longer a problem. If it had been a mile race and Strand, having passed the 1,500 metres line in his world record-equalling time of 3m. 43s, continued to run another 119 yards in 16.9 seconds that, at the time he felt fully capable of doing, he would have become the first sub-four-minute miler. This, I suggest, is also plausible. Breaking both the 1,500 metres record and that for the mile in the same race is hardly unknown (as Landy later demonstrated).

An awareness of the circumstances of Strand's 1,500 metres record shows that the benefits gained by Bannister were contingent on past athletic performances. There are several counterfactual outcomes to this perfectly plausible virtual history. First, obviously Bannister's 1954 mile – if he had run it – would not have been seen as nearly so remarkable. The four-minute mile, having been run in 1946, would not have been so worthy when it was subsequently run in 1954. Second, if the four-minute mile was no longer a magical target and, as Bannister claimed to be having increasing difficulties combining medicine and athletics, it is plausible that he would have retired from serious running after the disappointment of his Olympic fourth place in 1952. Third, Bannister's lack of association with the first four-minute mile and the absence of the related cultural capital, would have had non-athletic effects on his later life(style).

Such a brief counterfactual history illustrates how, when writing about sports stars, too much importance is sometimes attributed to the individual (in this case, Bannister) in the overall historical process (in this case, the history of the world mile record). My outline of Strand's earlier exploit tends to put Bannister more firmly in his place. Additionally, the last couple of paragraphs also illustrate how delicately balanced is a sporting reputation such as Bannister's. No one is 'born' to be a great runner. Such a virtual history makes Bannister's achievement look more modest and less heroic. I am drawn to the words of Argentinian anthropologist Eduardo Archetti: 'Heroes are normal beings who just do the right thing at precise moments'. Running 3m. 59.4s 46 days later would have been too late.

Had Strand run the first four-minute mile, Gordon Pirie would have been the most likely person to steal Bannister's thunder. A three-time

Olympian (Helsinki, Melbourne and Rome), conqueror of Vladimir Kuts and the world 5,000 metres record on a rain-soaked track in Bergen in a stunning time, and breaker of numerous British records, Pirie was esteemed by many people but never obtained the prestige that was bestowed on Bannister.

Roger Bannister was not all that different from other runners who preceded him, nor from several of his contemporaries. It is hard to see him as the 'gentleman amateur' and it is hard to see the four-minute mile as anything but a performance that was due to take place – and almost did take place in 1946. It is also difficult to see him as an unambiguous hero. He was criticised as much as he was praised.

My general reading re-presents Bannister as a man who displayed a strong sense of 'the modern' through his training, record-seeking and achievement orientation. Using the word in a non-literal way, he could be labelled a 'professional'. Lincoln Allison writes that 'professionals in any field are likely to err in the direction of caution, conformity and self-interest', when compared to the amateur. However, these were the very qualities that characterised the amateur athletic career of Roger Bannister. He displayed caution (he didn't race very often), he was conformist and a conservative (in the sense that he trained by adopting the conventional method of interval running), and appeared to display a considerable degree of self-interest. But it was modernism in moderation, professionalism in part; he did not take sport to excess. There was more to running than 'just slogging at training'. He did not want to run faster than he had to. He displayed 'amateur' traits, to the extent that he did not need to remain in running as he was able to tap in to other sources for self-esteem. His diversified life-history has arguably made him more 'normal' than those sports stars who are seemingly trapped, unable to ever leave the world of sports.

Simple dualisms like 'amateur' and 'professional' are not all that helpful in looking at Roger Bannister who turns out, it seems, to have been a sort of professional amateur. As far as his sporting life was concerned, enough was enough. He may have been aware of something that Nurmi and Lovelock (neither of whom seem to have been happy men) were not – that you can pay a terrible price for spending all your formative years working towards a distant and transient event. With his retirement from foot-racing he was freed from the body whose regimen had imprisoned him.

BIBLIOGRAPHIC NOTES

The context and details of Roger Bannister's sporting life are recorded in his own book, *First Four Minutes* (Putnam's, London, 1955; Sutton, Stroud, 2004), published in the USA as *The Four-Minute Mile* (Globe Pequot Press, Guilford, CT, 1981). Hardly surprisingly, the great majority of the quotations that I attribute to Roger Bannister are taken from this book. Additionally I have selectively included some of his responses to various interviews. Of considerable value is one with Brian Lenton in his collection, *Through the Tape* (Brian Lenton Publications, Duffy, ACT, 1983). This also includes an interview with Franz Stampfl. A lengthy and more recent interview is found at The Hall of Sports, *Interview with Roger Bannister*, (http://www.achievement. org/autodoc/page/ban0int-1?rand = 6427). A much briefer, but also recent, interview with James M. Clash adds some very minor details (http://www.forbes.com/lifestyle/collecting/2003/10/21/cz_jc_ 1021sport.html). Other observations by Bannister are found in his contributions to edited works such as two by H.A. Meyer, *Athletics* (Dent, London, 1958) and *Modern Athletics* (Oxford University Press, London, 1964) in which Norris McWhirter also has a chapter. Additionally, I have alluded to Bannister's comments in the *Olympic Bulletin*, 1954 and *The Listener* of the same year. More references to Stampfl are found in chapter 2 of Werner Reiterer, *Positive!* (Pan Australia, Melbourne, 2000) and in Stampfl's own book, *On Running* (Herbert Jenkins, London, 1958) in which Bannister pens an introduction.

Bannister's Oxford is well outlined by several chapters in volume 8 of *The History of the University of Oxford*, edited by Brian Harrison (Clarendon Press, Oxford, 1994), particularly that on 'Sport' by D.J. Wenden. Oxford in an earlier decade, and the place of athletics in Oxford culture, is also explored (sometimes imaginatively) by James McNeish, *Lovelock* (Godwit, Auckland, 1994). The history of Oxford University Athletics Club is found in Graham Tanner, *History of OUAC*, (http://users.ox.ac.uk/~ouac/page60.html). Amateurism in UK athletics is reviewed in Martin Polley's chapter in Adrian Smith and Dilwya Porter (eds), *Amateurs and Professionals in British Sport* (Frank Cass, London, 2000).

The history of the four-minute mile is subsumed in a number of histories of sports. There are many approaches. Statistical studies of the progress of the world mile record are included in Jay Bennett (ed.), *Statistics in Sport* (Arnold, London, 1998), T. Dwyer and K.F. Dyer, *Running out of Time: An Examination of the Improvement in Running Records* (New South Wales University Press, Kensington, NSW, 1984), Alphonse Juilland, *Rethinking Track and Field* (SEP Editrice, Milan, 2002), Ekkehard zur Megede, and Richard Hymans (eds), *Progression of World Best Performances and Official IAAF Records* (IAAF, Monaco, 1995). Dedicated fans can consult Bob Sparks, *Sub-4 Register in Date\Sequence*, (http://easyweb.easynet.co.uk/~rsparks/sub4-dat.htm). A very different approach that uses transcribed interviews with four-minute milers – including Landy but not Bannister – is adopted by Jim Denison, *Bannister and Beyond: An Oral History of the Four-Minute Mile* (Breakaway Books, Halcottsville, NY, 2003). An earlier, more conventional overview is found in George Smith, *All out for the Mile* (Forbes Robertson, London, 1955), but the definitive overview is Bob Phillips, *3:59.4: The Quest for the Four-Minute Mile* (Parrs Wood Press, Manchester, 2004). Chris Chataway's recollections of 1954 are in his article, 'The

Pacemaker' in *Prospect* (December 2003) while a somewhat unusual approach is adopted by Peter and Paul Stanley in their *The First Four Minute Mile and Tom Hulatt of Tibshelf* (Descartes Publishing, Peterborough, 2003). References to the first four-minute mile are also made in interviews conducted and transcribed by John Bromhead and housed in the British Athletics Archive in the library (special collections) at Birmingham University. I have consulted the interviews with Norris McWhirter and Phillip Noel-Baker. An interview with Roger Bannister was missing from the collection on the two occasions that I sought it from the archive.

Good histories of track and field athletics are few and far between. Many give the appearance of statistical gazetteers. The best of these works, in my view, is Roberto Quercetani, *Athletics: A History of Modern Track and Field Athletics, 1860–2000* (SEP Editrice, Milan, 2000). Early histories of track and field are more literary. In writing this book I have referred to what might be regarded as the canon, Montague Shearman, *Athletics and Football* (Longmans, Green, London, 1889). Interesting works from the inter-war period include S.A. Mussabini, *Running, Walking and Jumping* (Foulsham, London, 1926), Adolphe and Harold Abrahams, *Training for Athletics* (G. Bell, London, 1929), F.A.M. Webster, *Athletics Today: History, Development and Training* (Warne, London, 1929) and Arthur Newton, *Running* (Weatherly, London, 1935). These books are well supported by a well-written, though heavily statistical, work by Ross and Norris McWhirter, *Get to Your Marks!* (Nicholas Kaye, London, 1951). More recent athletics histories include Peter Lovesey, *The Official Centenary History of the AAA* (Guinness Superlatives, London, 1979), Edward S. Sears, *Running through the Ages* (McFarland, Jefferson, NC, 2001) and a delightful, visually stunning (but all too brief) book on Sydney Wooderson by David Thurlow, *Sydney Wooderson – Forgotten Champion* (self-published, no date). My information on Paavo Nurmi was gleaned from Veli-Matti Autio's essay in *The National Biography of Finland* (http://www.kansallisbiografia.fi/english.html) and the extensive English language appendix to Antero Raevuori, *Paavo Nurmi: Juoksijoiden Kuningas* (Werner Söderström, Porvoo, 1997).

On developments in training, excellent reviews are by Amby Burfoot, *The Evolution of Training Systems* (http://www.runnersworld.com/training/ evolution1.html). I also found Peter Mewett's chapter in C. Simpson and R. Gidlaw (eds), *Proceedings*: Australia and New Zealand Association of Leisure Studies Conference (Lincoln University, New Zealand, 1995) a good historical background to athletic training. For me, the best coverage of the athletic body is John Hoberman, *Mortal Engines* (The Free Press, New York, 1992). A broader, more 'scientific' approach is adopted in what is almost certainly the biggest book on running, the trans-disciplinary *Lore of Running* by Tim Noakes (Human Kinetics, Champaign, IL, 2003).

Histories of sport that take a broader view beyond athletics have been referred to in several cases. The standard text on British sports history is Richard Holt, *Sport and the British: A Modern History* (Clarendon Press, Oxford, 1989). This was followed up with Richard Holt and Tony Mason, *Sport in Britain 1945–2000* (Blackwell, Oxford, 2001). Both are excellent overviews and allude to Bannister's contribution. More sociologically inclined works on British sport have also often included references to Bannister. These include Lincoln Allison, *Amateurism in Sport* (Frank Cass, London, 2001), Andrew Blake, *The Body Language: The Meaning of Modern Sport* (Lawrence and Wishart, London, 1996) and two works by Garry Whannel, *Fields of Vision: Television, Sport and Cultural Transformation* (Routledge, London, 1992) and *Media Sports Stars: Masculinities and Moralities* (Routledge, London, 2002).

In this book I have only fleetingly engaged with 'historical method' but on 'social memory' I have consulted Chris Healy, *From the Ruins of Colonisation: History as Social Memory* (Cambridge University Press, Cambridge, 1997) and on the fascinating notion of 'virtual history' I referred to the standard work edited by Niall Ferguson, *Virtual History: Alternatives and Counterfactuals* (Pan, London, [1997] 2003). I am also indebted to Norman Denzin, *Interpretive Biography* (Sage University Paper Series on Qualitative Research Methods, vol. 17, Sage, Beverley Hills, CA, 1985) for his thoughts on 'layers of truth'.

Biographies and autobiographies of runners who were, more or less, contemporaries of Bannister have been useful in obtaining insights into Bannister's image. These works include Brian Hewson (with Peter Bird), *Flying Feet!* (Stanley Paul, London, 1962), Derek Ibbotson (with Terry O'Connor), *The Four-Minute Smiler* (Stanley Paul, London, 1960), Jim Peters, *In the Long Run* (Stanley Paul, London, 1956), Gordon Pirie, *Running Wild* (W.H. Allen, London, 1961), Graem Sims, *Why Die? The Extraordinary Percy Cerutty 'Maker of Champions'* (Lothian Books, South Melbourne, 2003) and Dick Booth's excellent biography of Gordon Pirie, *The Impossible Hero* (Corsica Press, London, 2000). A bewildering array of other material alludes to Roger Bannister. It would impossible to catalogue it all. Among the books that make passing, but interesting, references to him are Percy Cerutty, *Middle Distance Running* (Pelham, London, 1964).

On heroism I have been impressed with the writing of William J. Goode, *The Celebration of Heroes: Prestige as a Control System* (University of California Press, Berkeley, 1978) and with quite a different approach in Richard Holt's introductory essay to James Huntington-Whiteley, *The Book of British Sporting Heroes* (National Portrait Gallery, London, 1998). Further insights are found in *Sports Stars* edited by David Andrews and Steven Jackson (Routledge, London, 2001). I also consulted volume 45 of the journal *Quest*, for two interesting articles on sports heroes, one by Jeffrey Segrave and another by Alan Ingham, Jeremy Howell and Richard Swetman.

A number of sports (and other) journals and magazines have been consulted while writing this book. The most comprehensive coverage of Bannister's running career is found in *Athletics Weekly* (formerly *Athletics*, published monthly until about 1950), a mine of statistical information and public opinion about athletics and athletes. Another very important source, partly because its creators were close friends of Roger Bannister, is *Athletics World*, published by the McWhirter twins as a monthly from March 1952 to February 1957 as a labour of love. Arguably the best description of the four-minute mile, upon which I have drawn heavily, is found in the May 1954 issue. The American *Track and Field News* is another remarkable archive. Magazines covering a range of sports have featured Roger Bannister as both subject and author. *Sports Illustrated* is one, the now defunct *World Sports* is another.

Finally, I have referred at times to the notion of 'escape' in the context of Bannister's running. For anyone interested in escape I recommend Adam Phillips, *Houdini's Box: On the Arts of Escape* (Faber, London, 2001) and issue a challenge to apply Phillips's ideas to running.